C.L. THOMAS

DANCING WITH
DEMONS

A PARANORMAL ENCOUNTER

Second Edition

First Edition:
First printing

PUBLISHED BY CONNECTED UNIVERSE PRESS
A Division of HAUNTED ROAD MEDIA, LLC
www.hauntedroadmedia.com

Cleveland, Ohio
United States of America

ACKNOWLEDGMENTS

For those who encouraged me to keep moving forward.
The list is lengthy, and you know who you are.

Thank you.

TABLE OF CONTENTS

DAVE SCHRADER

Demonic forces, angry entities and dark energies exist.
Read that out loud to yourself and let it sink in.

The popularity of the paranormal is higher now than possibly any other time in history, and for the better part of the last twenty years has populated our televisions, streaming services and social media bringing us closer than ever, taking the stigma out of the closet and turning it into watercooler talk. With that said, the interest in the field of the paranormal and all things strange and unsettling has helped to open Pandora's box and release things we may never be able to put back in.

Now, more than ever, people have taken to investigating the paranormal as a hobby, calling forth spirits and entities in hopes of having an experience that they can walk away with, without the forethought that once you call things forward, there is little to do if they decide to attach themselves to a location or those investigating it, or worse yet, to those left behind to live in that haunted space and try to coexist with that energy.

Paranormal teams, for better or worse, have sprung up worldwide. Teams proclaim to have demonologists among their ranks, when in fact they have someone fascinated and self-taught by reading a few books and then proclaiming themselves to be the team demonologist or exorcist.

I cannot even begin to tell you the dangers that it creates. It would be no different than me proclaiming myself to be a physician because I watched hundreds of hours of procedural medical programs or claiming to be a stock car racer because I have seen every episode of The Dukes of Hazard and, like them Duke boys, I also drive a car.

A simple interest in a thing does not make you an expert. When it comes to working in a field where darkness is real, whether called forth, on purpose or by accident, there are real dangers to be considered, and not just to the investigative team or self-proclaimed demonologist. Their intrusion can, in fact, stir things up, make them worse and truly unleash holy hell.

Many of us dedicated to the field, to help both the living and the dead, are often called upon to sweep up the messes left behind by well-meaning teams or individuals that quickly realize they are in way over their heads and leave, and worse yet, make proclamations of demonic infestation as they scramble to their cars and their safe and distant homes, leaving the owners of the locations terrified, uncertain where to go and untrusting of calling upon another group for fear they will do the same or stir things up even further.

The story you are about to read is based on real people and experiences. It is frustrating, terrifying and overwhelming at times. This is how it is to deal with dark forces and commit to helping all involved. There are risks, physical, mental and spiritual, and Dear Readers, I pray you heed the warnings of dabbling in things you do not truly understand.

Demons are real. Where they emanate from is never an easy task to discern. We often want to blame Ouija boards, ancient burial grounds and historic battlefields, but sometimes, the darkness comes from within and feeds an already hungry entity. A person projecting fear, anxiety and loss of control can be responsible for unleashing dangerous forces without even realizing it. Even though we are several thousand years into calling forth spirits, holy people, witches, shamans and unseen forces, our knowledge of what we are truly tapping into is not yet fully realized. Sometimes it is guessing work, theories and following in the footsteps of those investigators that came before us to try to make sense of situations that are unfolding.

What I am trying to say is, show caution when moving forward into a field without any hard and fast answers. The thrill you seek may take root and upend your world. Ignorance is not always bliss; sometimes it is the key to a world of dangers unlike anything you could imagine. Author and dear friend, C. L. Thomas, has opened her heart to expose some very real, very scary details that I often wonder, has she ever gotten over. So, bear in mind that while reading a good, scary book can be entertaining, remember what you are about to read and the journey you are about to embark upon within these pages are based on real people, real circumstances and real repercussions of facing these types of hauntings.

My hope for you is that you and those you love never have to face this darkness or the demons that exist in reality and those we create in our minds. Walk safely, and I pray for protection for each one of you and those you love to be free of the misery, the isolation and pure abject terror that comes with hauntings such as you are about to read.

This is *Dancing with Demons.*

David Schrader

Lead investigator on Discovery Networks, The Holzer Files, Ghosts of Devil's Perch, The Curse of Lizzie Borden and host of The Paranormal 60 Podcast

October 11, 2023

Fr. KENNETH TORRES

As I reflect upon the profound and transformative pages that lie ahead, I am reminded of the timeless words of Carl Jung: "One does not become enlightened by imagining figures of light, but by making the darkness conscious." In the case of my dear friend, C.L. Thomas, the shadows cast by the paranormal have become a powerful catalyst for her healing and an invitation to explore the depths of the unseen.

In our world, where skepticism often reigns and the supernatural is met with doubt, it takes immense courage to delve into the realms beyond our ordinary perception. Yet, as a witness to C.L. Thomas's extraordinary journey, I can attest that this exploration has not only opened her eyes to a profound understanding of the unknown but has also paved the path toward her healing.

As a priest, I have guided others in their spiritual quests, offering solace and support in times of darkness. However, what C.L. Thomas presents within the pages of this remarkable book transcends the conventional boundaries of faith and dogma. It is a testament to the boundless potential of the human spirit and its ability to navigate ethereal realms.

Within these chapters, you will embark on a remarkable expedition into the supernatural and bear witness to C.L. Thomas's encounters with the paranormal. Her compelling narratives of inexplicable phenomena, harrowing battles, and astonishing revelations will challenge your preconceived notions and ignite a yearning for a deeper comprehension of the universe.

More than a mere chronicle of events, this book profoundly reflects on the transformative power of healing. It demonstrates how the unexplored territories of the paranormal can answer life's most perplexing questions and serve as a sacred gateway to personal growth and inner harmony.

As you journey alongside C.L. Thomas, allow her words to seep into your consciousness and stir the dormant embers of your curiosity. Embrace the fear and uncertainty that may arise as she recounts her encounters, for it is through acknowledging and confronting these elements that true transformation occurs.

This work may serve as a guiding light for all those who have experienced the mysterious and the otherworldly, and for those who are yet to explore the depths of the unknown. Let C.L. Thomas's story is a testament to the resilience of the human spirit and a reminder that healing is not confined to the boundaries of what we can see or understand.

With an open heart and an inquisitive mind, prepare to embark on a captivating odyssey that will challenge, inspire, and ultimately illuminate the path toward self-discovery and profound healing. As you turn each page, remember that the unseen has much to teach us, and it is within the shadows that we often find our greatest light.

May this book be a testament to the extraordinary power of the human spirit and an invitation to embrace the unseen.

Fr. Kenneth Torres, D.D.
Independent Catholic Clergy
www.fatherkendoctor.com

August 1, 2023

Encountering
– True Demonic Forces –

JAMES ANNITTO

Demons have held a significant place in human civilization since the inception of faith and religion. For there to be light, there must be darkness, and many within human society have acknowledged the dark aspects of life. Many have grappled with the internal struggle that tempts us towards wrongdoing, and for some, this struggle has led to eternal damnation. While this credible account of a paranormal encounter enlightens the masses, this demonic phenomenon is naturally beyond what one could truly comprehend.

Experiencing such phenomena is akin to believing in a boogeyman. Yet, when confronted with the boogeyman, it affects our livelihood, physical, and mental health. How can we overcome this? It's as if we must learn to dance with and against our evil partner to conquer this spiritual waltz. This struggle can span lifetimes or fleeting moments in our lives. The demonic masquerades and manipulates its way through deception, entrancing us with the unbelievable.

Terrifying accounts have been disseminated through

19

various forms of media and literature. However, within pop culture and society, we can see the influence of beings that despise and fall because of ourselves. One-third of the heavenly realm fell with the angel known as Lucifer, and now humans are falling more than ever, through various vices, through depression, etc. The light flickers as darkness grows.

This darkness is led by a non-corporeal force that preys, festers, and has existed longer than us. Hence, we might not understand the entire hierarchy or manifestations of beings from heavenly or hellish realms. Nonetheless, many have experienced it; many have survived to share their stories. As a Demonologist who has gazed into the eyes of the demoniac and been in the presence of the demonic, I can acknowledge their reality. However, encountering them is rarer than being struck by lightning. Nevertheless, just as lightning can strike an individual, so can the influence of the demonic, as discussed in this encounter by C.L. Thomas.

In my sixteen years of investigating and researching paranormal claims, I have encountered only five cases that could be categorized as Demonic from my perspective. Among those five, three involved possession, and the remaining two showed early stages of infestation and oppression. While some successfully separated from this diabolical force, others were not as fortunate, seeking different paths. Thus, as we progress in our spiritual dance, we must understand that once marked, an everlasting battle for the supremacy of our humanity may ensue.

James Annitto
Demonologist/Paranormal Investigator
www.jamesannitto.com

September 3, 2022

There is within us an extrasensory faculty that enables us, under certain conditions, to pierce the barriers of time and space.

Dr. Hans Holzer

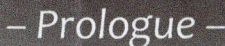

– Prologue –

THE ROOMMATE

Three of us sat on the floor, faint candlelight casting flickering shadows across the large room. We were in the master bedroom of our home, with an attached bathroom and walk-in closet that could easily house another roommate. To some extent, it did—just not the corporeal kind.

Nor the welcome kind.

We sat in front of a Ouija board as our guest called upon friendly spirits to help us find some peace. This attempt wasn't the first, nor the last, to rid our home of the unwanted inhabitant. It certainly didn't help much.

Our friend invoked the wisdom and protection of his deities. Again, it wasn't the first or last time anyone had performed such a ritual. Priests, priestesses, rabbis, saints, sinners, and witches had all tried their hand at banishing whatever tormented us.

And nothing seemed to work. An air of dread always lingered. Sometimes it would fade after a ritual or cleansing, but it always came back, angrier than before.

When I first moved in, I tried my damnedest to ignore it, but I could always feel it. Something would always catch my attention, even when I tried to pretend it didn't happen. I chalked it up to being in a new place—the first apartment I had post-college after living with my parents to save money.

I assumed the lease of a guy moving out to pursue life choices probably be better than mine in the long run. I had visited several times and moved in slowly as he moved out at the same speed. The place felt odd, but I thought it was simply because it was new to me. And slightly awkward because I felt like the former roommate was being rushed out by my presence.

But once he was gone, I tried to settle into my room and new surroundings. The property was fantastic. There was a community pool, it was close to my work and some of the best restaurants in town, and it was very quiet.

A creek rolled through the property, and occasionally, wildlife would visit. But other than that, and the faint hum of nearby traffic, the place was silent. It's the type of quiet you get used to. It's calming, and when something breaks it, everything shatters.

About a month after I moved in, I noticed something was going to shatter that peaceful experience. At first, I thought it was just my mind playing tricks on me. But the vision hung in my mind, even as I tried to push it out. It was a shadow at the end of the hall, right outside my bathroom and my roommate's door. And it slipped through the wall in the blink of an eye.

"The lighting is just bad there," I tried to tell myself. But I knew. I could feel it.

I've always been sensitive to the spiritual world, even though I'm not religious. When I was a child, I kept seeing people in my home through the corner of my eye or in fleeting glances. There was a man in the hallway—he went nowhere else in the house. A woman would flutter here and there, and so would another man. But it was the one in the hall that scared me.

My nights, starting around the age of nine, were plagued with terrifying dreams. Faces came out of walls and ceilings. Eyes glowed back through mirrors. Voices were everywhere. One time, I woke at our front door, screaming and then just confused. I was so terrified that I was trying to get out of the house.

Eventually, I couldn't tell what was real at night versus what was a nightmare. I became terrified of mirrors facing beds, something I haven't grown out of, but thanks to horrible vision, it hasn't been an issue. But those mirrors held spirits trapped by something, yearning to be free. One night, I sat up in my bed, not sure if I was awake or dreaming, and saw an image that haunts me to this day. The man in the hall was there, pointing at me with glowing red eyes and swinging back and forth.

Back and forth.

Back and forth.

I tried to scream, but no sound came out of my mouth. Suddenly, my mom was there, and everything was okay. I told her what I saw, and she said nothing.

It wasn't until I was an adult that I learned the family who lived there before us had all died in the house. The son had hung himself in the hallway where they found him swinging back and forth.

Back and forth.

It's an image that seared into my mind. While C.L. and I

were roommates, it danced in my memories as I saw that shadow figure in the hallway more often. I wondered if something had followed me, and that worry sometimes consumed me. But nothing had followed me. This being was very different from any I had encountered in my youth. I would think back to how other hauntings made me feel. Was I feeling those same sensations? Or was it just all in my head? Or was this something more sinister?

My history with C.L. and the supernatural didn't begin with moving into this home. In fact, it began much earlier. I met C.L. a few years before we became roommates. We would frequently go ghost hunting in cemeteries or other bizarre places and then make our way to a Mexican restaurant to discuss our findings. We had voice recorders, cameras, and an EMF detector. We wouldn't have even known about some of the tech out there if it hadn't been for T.V. shows that popularized ghost hunting. We were always careful not to bring anything back with us. We would do cleansings, say whatever prayers—anything. And it seemed to work.

Dear reader, I can say, without a doubt, that what was in our home did not come back with us from an adventure. It was unlike anything we encountered before or since.

I lost sleep. I had nightmares. Sometimes I'd sleep at a friend's house. I would turn up the TV and music subconsciously to hide sounds. I turned the lights on as bright as I could. I'd leave a light on in rooms I wasn't in—anything to not be in the dark. And I covered mirrors so I couldn't see what might look back at me.

My cat frequently stared at walls in that unsettling way cats do when they see something you really don't want them to. (One time, it was a mouse. The mouse died in the wall, and that was a smell that would rival whatever lived in our place with us.)

C.L. and I worked on different schedules. Oftentimes, she was asleep while I was leaving for work. Some of the paranormal activities I would just cast off as her being exhausted and forgetful from a long shift. For example, one morning, I walked into the kitchen to discover every cabinet and drawer open. I thought she had been looking for something and, in her exhaustion, didn't think about closing anything. Slightly absurd, yes?

I had no idea she hadn't gotten home yet. I wasn't one to go into her room at that point, though that would change when she got sick a few years later. I really had no idea she wasn't there until I went to leave and saw her car was gone.

At some point, denial becomes impossible. I asked her later if she had left the kitchen a mess. She said no. It was then I placed an electronic voice recorder in the kitchen and let it record while we were both away one day. The playback left us shaken. Cabinets slammed, footsteps paced, there was heavy breathing, and finally a growl that said, "GET OUT!"

It startled me. But I wasn't scared. I had already heard the voices, saw the shadows, felt cold spots, and experienced unexplained activity that just kept growing. We never knew what we would encounter each day. I started sleeping with the television on; so, did she. Anything to drown out the sounds. At some point, I noticed that C.L. was sleeping in her bedroom with her lamp on. She had gotten to the point where she would not sleep without the lamp off.

Things continued this way for a few months. We could not enjoy a night off without something happening in the house. There were several times in which we had movie nights in our living room with our cats, (we both owned cats, C.L had two and I had one) only to be interrupted by what sounded like an entire shelving system falling to the ground.

But every time, upon inspection, there was nothing. The activity was consistent, growing steadily as time went on.

Weeks went by, and neither of us were sleeping well. I was exhausted at work when C.L. called me in a panic, begging me to come home as she was terrified. The entity had tried to attack her cat. She saw unexplained events with her own eyes and was absolutely panicked. I told my boss my roommate was having an emergency. I was in overtime at that point, so leaving wasn't an issue. As I drove home, I started playing a scene in my mind of what to do. I called a friend for help.

This friend was sensitive, and she came over to offer help or guidance. She said she felt the presence of two very distinct beings. One was a man who wanted to peer in on her while she was in my bathroom—harmless but annoying. The other, she said, confirming my worst fears, was something much darker and in the room just next door. This story tells what happened behind that door, expanding into the entire home. A door opened that we could never close.

M.H.P.
The Roommate

INTRODUCTION

In a way, I grew up in the presence of ghosts. I began seeing the other side at such an early age that my very first memory is of an entity in my room. My childhood had a certain magic to it, as these beings would visit me and provide comfort when I needed it the most. When I sought distraction from the harsh realities of my troubled childhood, I found entertainment in balls of light floating around my crib.

Coming from a dysfunctional home, I learned the art of dissociation early on, enabling me to perceive the other side more readily than most. Some might easily dismiss this as psychosis, or merely imaginary friends; however, since I've had more than one witness to strange events throughout my life, it's hardly dismissible. I grew up seeing people who had passed away and could describe them without ever having met them before. I also had knowledge of facts that I shouldn't have been able to perceive.

This book is written for those who have struggled in their lives with supernatural events, negative energy attachments, and the consequences of having psychic abilities. Part of this book discusses a neighbor whom I believe opened a gateway through ritualistic work. This by no means implies that I condone practitioners of any form of witchcraft or other practices. This neighbor has done nothing wrong but may have inadvertently opened a doorway into our house. This book is not written to endorse or disprove any specific religion, including Catholicism. When I mentioned my disagreement with the priest blessing the house in this book, it simply meant that it wasn't the right approach for that situation.

I firmly believe that everyone can connect with a source outside of themselves, beyond the bounds of time and space. We all have the ability to perceive through Extrasensory Perception (ESP). Some may have this talent more readily than others, but we all have it, nonetheless. No one can claim to be the sole conduit to the realm of angelic beings, ancestors, and the like. Spirit is just a heartbeat away. The paranormal will always remain a mystery, and there are no true experts in this field.

This work explores the possible correlation between suicide and demonic activity and explores the idea that negative entities can play havoc on someone's physical energy and mental state. The actual house that is discussed in this book is owned by an investor, and as agreed, will be kept private. Some of the names mentioned have been changed to protect their privacy rights.

The bible suggests that the struggle of man against evil influences is the whole history of the world. This inference creates all literature and ancient religions. Arthur Crane writes in *The Great Exorcism* that "they (negative entities) fasten themselves gradually upon you, bring dreams and imaginings, seem to set the rest of the world against you, and torment you into insanity and death."

This is my story and personal encounter of a hostile haunting almost ten years ago that forever changed me. I try to bring to light how destructive demonic and negative attachments are, particularly for those who are overly interested in having a "paranormal experience." *Dancing with Demons* has been a complicated piece to write for many reasons.

The purpose of writing this book is to inspire those who may be grappling with spiritual struggles and paranormal experiences to look upward. Energy surrounds us, and we can choose how we respond to it or whether we pay attention to it at all. My journey has been long, and I've learned a great deal in a short amount of time. I've burned many bridges in the process of learning how to Dance with the Demons, without being overcome by them. But it's also been a great lesson on how to take back my power and move forward in life.

– Chapter 1 –

A PLACE IN NASHVILLE

"The spirit of evil was from the beginning bent upon man's destruction." – **Unknown**

During my first visit to the house that would reshape my perspective on the paranormal during a leasing tour, everything seemed unremarkable except for the picturesque, serene creek winding alongside the spacious porch, reminiscent of a veranda. This porch featured three sets of French doors, providing access to every room in the house. The house didn't look out of the ordinary, nor did it even look old. At the time, I was not looking for ghosts. But for some inexplicable reason, ghosts always seemed to find me.

To tell this story, I need to go back to where it all started. My first paranormal encounter for me happened at a very young age. One of the first memories I have is of a spirit figure in my room. Most people have no memory of themselves in a baby crib, but I do. There was a time when I crawled out of my crib to play with another child spirit. On several occasions, an elderly man figure stood guard over my crib. And strange balls of light would bounce around the room, keeping me occupied from the noise outside of the closed door.

It extended beyond merely having imaginary companions. These spirits not only served as my friends but also assumed protective roles when needed. From early on, my innocence as a child was lost to my parents' emotional maelstrom. On many nights, loud, harsh voices boomed like thunderstorms, accompanied by furniture crashing and glass breaking. Being raised in a dysfunctional household meant that, regardless of how long I cried, there was no one coming to soothe me in my crib. Maybe it was this early dissociation to protect myself that drew me closer to the spirit world. Like me, there are many people who report certain mediumship abilities after trauma.

There was one spirit in particular, the elderly man, during that period of my life that became a guardian to some degree. He resembled an elderly gentleman, with a full white beard and rotund belly. To a small child, he looked to be a large man, like the fictional character Rubeus Hagrid in the *Harry Potter* book series written by J. K. Rowling. He was not a frightening figure but had a more comforting nature toward me.

I was still young enough to sleep in a crib, but old enough to somehow connect this gentleman to a name that seemed familiar to me. Oddly enough, I called this figure Santa, after the Santa Claus figure in the 1964 classic movie, *Rudolph the Red-Nose Reindeer*. This spirit would appear in front of the doorway on nights when the frightening was bad, as if somehow shielding me from the troubles outside of the door. The connection between this spirit as "Santa" was remarkable in historical meaning this connotation alludes to. Traditionally, Santa Claus represented a jolly mythical figure in the guise of a man, who was the protector of children in need. The true story of the Santa Claus figure we have today is from a legend surrounding the life of Bishop Nicholas in the first century, who became known throughout the land for his generosity to those in need, his love for children, and his concern for sailors and ships. This Saint was even believed to have healing powers after his death! St. Nicholas appeared to a terrified boy named Basilios, who had been kidnapped by ruthless assailants with the intention of selling him into slavery. St. Nicholas blessed him and safely returned him to his home This is the first story told of St. Nicholas, the modern-day Santa Claus, protecting children—which became his primary role in the West. There is no way a child my age at the time could have made this connection.

Many mediums have dramatic tales of spirits haunting them throughout their childhood and speak about how frightened they were. I'm not suggesting that this is mere melodrama by any means, but this wasn't my earlier experience with the paranormal. The spirit realm felt entirely commonplace to me from a very young age to the extent that I remained oblivious to the societal expectation that the living should fear it. Although there were times when I was startled by paranormal activity as a child, I never truly feared it. The first time I ever feared a spirit was while living in a house in Nashville, Tennessee.

During that day's property tours, I found myself alone since my partner was occupied with clinical duties. We needed a place to live, but his clinical rotation prevented him from taking part in securing a place. Instructions were, if it made me happy and looked "quiet" then begin the leasing process and he would take care of having our stuff moved. We aimed to complete our move by the end of the month, and since it was already the second week of the month, I was feeling the pressure of a tight schedule. During my initial visit, stepping inside the house for the first time yielded no hints about what lay hidden beneath the surface. The vintage facade, complete with a welcoming veranda, exuded a charming Southern allure, complemented by the gentle murmur of the brook flowing past the porch. At first glance, there was no indication that this house was haunted. Reflecting on the experience, it's clear that the mere presence of history or historical significance does not imply it's haunted. Though I experienced many paranormal events during my childhood, I was not seeking the paranormal. Such events experienced in my childhood and beyond lay silent in the forgotten shadows of my mind as I pursued an education. Yet, the paranormal sought me out and found me in this ordinary rental house in South Nashville, Tennessee.

At that time, my partner was a sporty, blond individual pursuing a doctorate in sports medicine and physical therapy at the same university as me. Our schedules were packed; he juggled clinicals and classes during the day, while I worked and attended night classes. We had been in a relationship for nearly six months and were taking the significant step of moving in together. To the outside world, we appeared to be the perfect match, with everything seemingly falling into place. Together, we explored the wooded trails in our surroundings, making a pact to conquer every great hike in the Middle Tennessee area. We engaged in playful banter, relished life, and both had promising careers ahead in the medical field. It's remarkable how swiftly life can change in the blink of an eye, and our journey together took a different turn as soon as we signed a lease and stepped into the unsettling, ominous house.

By the time we settled into our new rental house, I was

still quite new to Nashville, having departed from my life in Pennsylvania just months prior in a quest for self-improvement, following a turbulent family experience. My ambitions were to attain a prestigious degree, heal from the abuse endured in a dysfunctional home, and forge a better path for myself than my parents had. As I left home, I was initially utterly shattered and emotionally overwhelmed by the events that had unfolded there. The emotional turmoil clung to me for many years as I tried to escape the fear and uncertainty that lingered and to discover a path toward relief and freedom.

In those days, Nashville was a far cry from the city it has become today. Nashville hot chicken was not a trend, although the original Nashville Hot Chicken place, Prince's, existed in a rundown and unsafe area off Nolensville Pike. Much of Nashville was run down back then, and the infamous 12 South Neighborhood was not safe enough for a stroll after dark, particularly around the now-famous Sevier Park, which has transformed into a popular neighborhood outdoor music venue in recent years. Five Points in East Nashville was too unsafe even to consider renting an apartment, let alone establishing a trendy eatery. No one knew at the time that all of this would change within a decade.

In the past, Downtown Nashville didn't possess the magnetic appeal it boasts today among tourists and visitors. Back then, the city's skyline showcased the Bat Building, which has since become an enduring symbol of Nashville. Alongside it stood several towering office buildings, such as the Pinnacle at Symphony Place, the Fifth Third Center, and the SunTrust Plaza. These skyscrapers played a vital role in shaping the city's burgeoning urban landscape, marking a transition toward a more metropolitan Nashville.

During those days, the nightlife scene in the downtown area was rather limited, with only a handful of renowned bars dotting the infamous Broadway Boulevard. These establishments catered primarily to the music shows taking place at the Ryman Auditorium. Iconic venues like Tootsie's, the Ugly Coyote, Robert's, and Legends Corner, historic honky-tonks nestled along Broadway, had already cemented their status as integral fixtures in the downtown Nashville scene, drawing in patrons for many years. The present-day Nashville Scene bears only faint echoes of its earlier incarnation, characterized by the music emanating from its bars, which featured singer-songwriters and artists. Today, the soundscape has largely shifted to club music, cover bands, and revelers catering to a steady stream of bridal parties.

As a newcomer to the South, I found myself navigating a culture that made me feel like a stranger in a foreign land, unmistakably branded as a "Yankee in the South." I was entirely unfamiliar with the South, particularly the elongated vowels and the relaxed way people spoke. In contrast, my partner, hailing from Michigan, had already become proficient in the Southern dialect. He had previously relocated from the New Orleans area during his research on turtle preservation in the bayous before shifting his focus to sports medicine. This novel dialect left me wrestling with its meaning, for I had not yet grasped the nuances of words like "fixin'," "polecats," or the genteel manner of expressing sympathy, encapsulated in the phrase "bless her heart." In the northeastern part of the United States, my former home of Pittsburgh, Pennsylvania, "fixin'" meant something was broken, "polecats" were the stars of late-night dance floors, and offering a blessing to someone was always a gesture of goodwill. I would encounter that last term repeatedly as I tried to navigate my way through the trials and tribulations of a new, unfamiliar region of the United States.

A whole new world had opened before me, replete with abandoned houses nestled deep within forests, antebellum plantations standing in all their former grandeur, and a profound history that ran as deep as an unhealing wound. Moreover, nearly every town harbored dark tales of mayhem, from pirates and soldiers' legends to remote plantations owned by madmen, towns constructed atop the resting places of the deceased, and eerie accounts of hauntings in the bayous, Civil War battlefields, and even at enigmatic crossroads amidst forsaken cotton fields. I was immediately captivated.

One of my first, peculiar nighttime excursions in the South occurred by chance. A fellow colleague had mentioned that deep within the old-growth trees of Percy Warner Park, a type of lichen clinging to the sides of overgrown hackberry and oak trees, thriving among the rocks beneath the canopy, possessed the ability to glow in the dark. So, armed with flashlights on a late Friday night, we parked our cars along Belle Meade Boulevard, crossed the chain intended to deter nighttime vehicles, and trekked through the damp woods, accompanied by the sounds of peeper frogs and barred owls. We were in pursuit of the enigmatic bioluminescent moss. The thrilling experience of seeking the unknown drew me, growing into bigger mysteries, seeking legends and lore.

During the first month in the house, there were no unusual occurrences. I spent my early spring days exploring the expansive landscapes of towering trees and historic plantations, with minimal time spent indoors. My fascination lay with the intricately constructed stone walls, painstakingly crafted by former slaves who hand-cut each piece of limestone and skillfully fitted them together, forming four-foot-high walls that delineated the property boundaries of previous landowners before the Civil War. These stone walls extended for miles, some still demarcating the borders of properties that had long faded into obscurity, now cutting through overgrown forests.

The specters of the Civil War permeated every corner. I even unearthed these apparitions in the shape of Civil War bullets while tending to my garden at home. To intensify our search for discarded cannonballs along the creek that meandered by our house, we invested in a Garrett model metal detector. As it happened, our house sat upon the very ground where the Battle of Nashville had raged. A Tennessee historical marker stood proudly along Franklin Pike, a mere hundred meters from our doorstep.

However, the house itself did not share this history and was constructed long after the war had ended. The area's history became a source of fascination for me as I delved into accounts of Nashville falling into Union hands and the bloody battles that unfolded throughout the region. Indeed, many of the older locals still clung to the belief that the war persisted, as evidenced by their display of rebel flags atop their houses. Just down the road from our house on Franklin Pike, a lawyer erected a twelve-foot statue in honor of Nathaniel Bedford Forrest, visible from the interstate. This statue had long been a contentious eyesore for the city until a vandal finally tore it down, but not without first dousing it in buckets of red paint in the dead of night.

As the early Spring months warmed up, subtle occurrences started to unfold around the house, so subtle that though they curiously caused me some concern, they were easily waved away. Items would seemingly move, such as keys turning up where they weren't placed, and in one instance, I found a purse in a completely different room from where I had left it. One could easily argue that I misplaced the bag and forgot where I set it down. However, living with a guy that was particular about where things should go, it was a daily habit that things had a proper place, and this practice never deviated.

It went beyond my familiarity with the history that surrounded me. It all started with the faintest shadow darting across the hallway in my peripheral vision and the eerie sensation of being watched by an unseen phantom. These subtle events reopened a door to the paranormal world, a realm I believed I had left behind in my youth. I was aware of the presence of spirits, and I couldn't help but be drawn to it. Or, perhaps, were they drawn to me?

My partner, an avid skeptic and scientist, dismissed the unusual happenings as mere coincidences. Even the concept of God was too steeped in superstition for him to find any value in it. To him, religion appeared as a construct designed to maintain control over humanity, manipulated by dictators and rulers throughout history. In some respects, he had a point. Regrettably, matters of the spirit have often been exploited for centuries to serve the interests of specific groups of people.

Some individuals cling to existence with the fear that this earthly life is all there is. However, this perspective doesn't negate the presence of the spiritual realm for those who have experienced it firsthand. Those who deny the existence of the spiritual often seem to carry a deep-seated emptiness or sense of hopelessness within them.

Within just a few months of living in the house, a noticeable shift occurred between us. The once positive and cheerful man I had initially met gave way to a brooding, angry personality. He became increasingly isolated, retreating

41

deep into himself, burdened by bitterness over things from the past that he couldn't control or release. Our hikes turned into speed contests, and even the simplest meals triggered petty arguments. One night, his enraged outburst from the guest bathroom startled me awake. He claimed to have seen something in the hallway but refused to divulge any further details. Clearly tormented by whatever force he believed he was contending with, he embarked on a solitary nighttime walk that week. During the same period, he moved in with a mutual friend from the University. In response, I invited another friend to occupy the spare bedroom. It became evident that I needed to exit the relationship, not just for his sake but for my own well-being. We were traversing different life paths and seeking different futures. Much like the shifts in the house's paranormal activity, the winds of seasonal change abruptly altered my personal life.

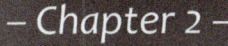

– Chapter 2 –

A GATEWAY

**"The spirit of evil was from the begin
O Moon that rid'st the night to wake
Before the dawn is pale,
The hamadryad in the brake,
The Satyr in the vale,
Caught in thy net of shadows
What dreams hast thou to showing
bent upon man's destruction."
– Gerald B. Gardner**

Now that my boyfriend moved out, the winds of change swept through my life, not only reshaping my personal world but also casting a curious light on the supernatural occurrences within our home. My attention shifted as my best friend settled into the guest room, drawing me into her vibrant world. Hailing from East Nashville, she introduced me to a whirlwind of friends and family over the course of those initial weeks. Our once silent and somber abode was now alive with the sounds of music and laughter, thanks to the housewarming parties we hosted. My new roommate, a college colleague and fellow history enthusiast, led me on a captivating journey through the historical treasures of Nashville and the charming town of Franklin. Because of her background, she was familiar with all the legends of the area, and so we explored the various sites consisting of dark tales and folklore.

One such place that quickly became a favorite because of the haunting lore around it is the Belmont Mansion, constructed in 1849 on the grounds of Belmont University, where we both attended. It was an antebellum estate once owned by one of the largest slave trade owners in the United States, Adelicia Acklen. The grounds surrounding the mansion, which now houses the main offices of Belmont University, featured elegant gardens, a lake with a water tower, a large bathhouse, a luxurious conservatory, and a man-made lake.

Adelicia is said to still haunt the grounds in eternal retribution for her role in the cruelty of the slave trade industry. However, despite the benefits and wealth her trade afforded her, it came at a steep price. After losing a former fiancé and two husbands, she went on to lose six of her young children to malaria. Her first marriage is shrouded in misfortune and death. At the age of twenty-two, Adelicia married Isaac Franklin, a wealthy businessman and plantation owner who was twenty-eight years her senior. Isaac and Adelicia had four children together, all of whom died before the age of eleven. Isaac Franklin himself died unexpectedly of a stomach virus while visiting one of his plantations in Louisiana.

Strange tales and legends of sightings of the Lady of Belmont continue to circulate among various staff and students on campus, especially around a full moon. Every year, Adelicia was known to host a grand ball, which was always held during a full moon, to allow the visitors to see her wealth and her mansion in all its glory. At Belmont, she entertained such notables as President Andrew Johnson, inventor Alexander Graham Bell, socialite Octavia La Vert, philosopher Thomas Huxley and soldier of fortune William Walker, as well as numerous Confederate officers and political figures.

Stories such as these drew me ever closer to the paranormal world. Together, my new roommate and I toured many of the plantation houses around the surrounding counties and dove into the darker legends that my roommate knew from growing up here. I was fascinated. The activity around our own house was still subtle, if not quiet at first. I told my roommate about some shadows I would catch from the corner of my eye, or the fleeting feeling that someone else was in the room with us. But these occurrences were so subtle that they were hardly worth mentioning, at first. This would quickly change within just a few weeks of my friend getting settled in the house.

As the summer solstice approached, I found myself tumbling deeper into the enigmatic realm of the paranormal. Eerie occurrences, each one stoking my curiosity, began to dominate the atmosphere within our house. Meanwhile, beyond our walls, the world shimmered under the oppressive weight of sweltering heat and stifling humidity. The impending summer solstice loomed on the horizon, casting a spell of anticipation over the land. As daylight stretched its sinewy fingers longer and longer each day, the world braced itself for the sun's triumphant zenith, promising endless hours of golden warmth and whispered secrets carried on the breeze. It was a time when shadows shrunk to their smallest, and the earth seemed to hold its breath in eager anticipation of the longest day, when the sun would reign supreme in the cerulean sky.

In Nashville, we collectively held our breath for another annual event: the notorious locusts returning after seven years. Within a matter of days, hordes of large black cicadas with beady red eyes emerged from the ground, crawling out in the hundreds, as if demons were rising from the depths of hell itself, ready to wreak havoc on anyone in their path. In the garden, the tranquil sounds of the creek and frogs were drowned out by the deafening cacophony of these buzzing insects. What had been lush and damp just a week ago was now overrun by cicadas. They were drawn to the roar of engines, swarming, and clogging air conditioning units, and launching relentless assaults on moving lawnmowers. Despite my deep dislike for these insects, my personal life had grown strangely quiet with the absence of the violent arguments and heated discussions that had plagued my relationship with my ex-partner. However, as the cicada brood settled noisily in the trees around my house, a more sinister presence seemed to lurk within, waiting for the perfect moment to reveal itself.

Once my roommate had settled in and my heart had begun to heal, even if only slightly, from the recent breakup and loss, we fell into a regular routine. This routine was occasionally disrupted by the initially subtle paranormal occurrences that started to become more frequent within the house.

Over the next several weeks, an energy akin to static seemed to permeate the house, demanding our attention, and steadily intensifying. It began with a slow rotation, accompanied by fleeting shadows, peculiar sounds that initially elicited mere shrugs, lights flickering or dimming, and my cat's unexplained dashes away from phantom specters in the hallway or the walk-in closet in the master suite. As the weeks passed, this energy quickened its spin, reminiscent of the formation of a storm.

A lengthy, shallow hallway extended from the front of the house to its farthest end, ultimately leading to the master bedroom—my bedroom. My bedroom suite resembled its own miniature apartment. It boasted a queen-sized bed, an entertainment center, bookshelves, a cozy couch, and a dedicated desk area. Even with all these furnishings, there remained ample space in the center for me to perform yoga routines. Adjoining this expansive suite was a generously sized bathroom, complete with a set of his and hers sinks and a luxurious soaking tub.

In this suite, the walk-in closet occupied the furthest corner from the house's entrance and shared a wall with the neighboring apartment. An unmistakable energy seemed to converge within that walk-in closet, along the shared wall with the adjacent apartment. This led us to believe that the entity favored this location for concealment, occasionally passing through the shared wall into the neighboring apartment.

Considering that this space had once formed a single residence, it was conceivable that a doorway had existed there in the past. Strangely, while searching for a missing shoe that I believed had become lodged beneath the bottom shelf, I stumbled upon a small wooden crucifix hidden in the far corner of the closet, wedged between the shelf and the baseboard against the wall. This discovery prompted me to keep the closet and bathroom doors closed. My bed was positioned to face the doorway, and on certain nights, I imagined I glimpsed swift, dark four-foot shadows darting across the bathroom through the doorway. To this day, I remain uncertain whether those shadows were mere optical illusions or tangible entities, given the abundance of paranormal activity that occurred during that time.

It didn't take long for my new roommate to have her first encounter with the paranormal. She started reporting sightings of shadows in her bathroom, which happened to be the main bathroom of the house. These were the same fleeting, four-foot shadows that I frequently observed in my own bathroom. She also began noticing that objects would topple over on the bathroom sink, or items would mysteriously appear in different locations from where she had left them.

On another occasion, she was overwhelmed by the sensation that someone else was present in the bathroom while she was taking a shower. Terrified, she hastily grabbed her towel and stepped into a chilling cold spot during her otherwise steam-filled bathroom. As time passed, the activity appeared to intensify with each new experience.

One weekend while I was away, she had a chilling experience in her bedroom. Alone in the dimly lit room, she suddenly heard an eerie disembodied female voice emanating from the long hallway. Interestingly, this was the same area where my recent partner had spotted a shadow just a few weeks earlier. Her bedroom was situated across the hallway from a spacious bathroom she often used. With her bedroom door ajar, she had a partial view of the bathroom. To her astonishment, the voice made a return appearance just a few nights later, jolting her awake. She described it as the voice of a woman speaking in the hallway, though the words were indecipherable. Initially, she thought it might be me, but I was not at home during that time. Bewildered, she meticulously inspected the house, ensuring she was truly alone. She double-checked that all the doors and windows were securely shut and then returned to bed, attributing the mysterious voice to a possible neighbor next door. However, as similar instances occurred repeatedly, it became clear that no sounds ever emanated from the neighboring apartment. Our shared realization was that the source of these unsettling occurrences remained a haunting mystery.

Shortly after her first genuine paranormal encounter in the house, I was roused from slumber during the early morning hours by a similar experience. It was the predawn hour, a time when inexplicable activity seemed to intensify each night for the next several months. The sounds of movement in the kitchen reached my ears, akin to someone preparing a late-night meal. Pots and pans clanged as they were shuffled about, and there was the distinct clatter of a pot settling onto the stove, followed by the clinking of one plate against another, accompanied by rhythmic sound of a wooden spoon stirring in a metal pan.

I lay there, half-asleep, pondering why my roommate was cooking so late into the night and making such a clamor. Then, a sudden realization struck me—I detected no savory aroma, despite the sounds that typically accompanied culinary endeavors. With reluctance, I rose from my bed, embarked down the dimly lit hallway, and saw that my roommate was fast asleep in her room. The end of the corridor remained shrouded in darkness, revealing no signs of anyone in the kitchen. Switching on the hallway light, I traversed through the dining room and entered the kitchen, which proved to be eerily untouched. No pots and pans lay scattered about, and the porcelain plates I had heard clinking against the countertop were safely nestled in the cabinet. The kitchen was impeccably orderly, untouched since the previous evening.

As the paranormal activity escalated, my fascination with

the supernatural was reignited. Long-buried memories of childhood encounters started to surface once more. Growing increasingly curious about the phenomenon, we sought answers through cable television. At the time, there were limited resources available, as discussions about the paranormal were still rare. Fortunately, a handful of TV shows had begun to air. *Ghost Hunters*, which was already in its second season, along with *A Haunting* and the British series *Most Haunted*, were the only outlets willing to delve into the paranormal landscape a mere decade ago. For a month or two, it became a regular Friday ritual for us to prepare dinner after work and indulge in these shows. However, we soon began to realize that even this innocent routine was somehow contributing to the peculiar energy within the house. A factor that came into play was that the shows turned us onto the idea of investigating our house and collecting evidence, which in turn, would feed the paranormal activity with our attention.

Investigating was a turning point in my interest in the paranormal, especially when I learned about the use of equipment by watching the television paranormal investigators. One of the most significant "aha" moments we gleaned from the Sci-Fi show *Ghost Hunters* was the utilization of small security cameras and digital recorders. I was in graduate school at the time and happened to have a pocket-sized Sony recorder on my desk. Inspired by the show, I decided to begin recording various locations in the house by simply leaving it on while I went out. Initially, the recorder only captured rustling sounds, minor bangs, and occurrences that could easily be attributed to the air conditioning unit or even possibly my twenty-pound Burmese cat I owned skirting through the room. However, over time, we also began to capture audible voices. The challenge with our approach was that it consumed a considerable amount of time to review the extensive hours of recordings.

With both of us experiencing the activity in the house, we decided to try and contact whatever was causing the energy in the house, be it a ghost, or something else. We figured that if we made some sort of contact, that maybe we could figure out some sort of solution to the activity to make it stop. First, we needed to figure out if the hauntings were caused by an intelligent spirit or if it was a residual in nature. Given the history of the land that we lived on, plus the water in the creek that ran past the house and even the limestone in the ground, we had to rule out the possibility of the activity being caused by tape theory.

Residual energy is often associated with locations where highly emotional or traumatic events have occurred, such as a battle ground on which we lived. It was possible that the energy was being played over and over by the running water in the creek, and some believe energy can be stored in limestone. We had to be sure, even though this theory did not support the poltergeist activity of objects moving about the house.

It was another hot and muggy night in June when we gathered in the dining room to conduct our investigation. Turning out all the lights and cell phones, we lit several candles that cast an eerie light around the room. I pressed the record button on the Sony recorder and placed it in the center of the dining table. We simply sat there, not sure what to say or even ask, just waiting in the quiet with bated breath. My heart pounded in my chest, and I half expected a shadow to run across the wall like they so often did. As I sat in silence, my gaze fixed on the flickering candlelight dancing along the walls, an eerie sensation washed over me—a palpable presence in the room. Closing my eyes, I focused on this inexplicable feeling. Images of a woman with dark hair flashed through my mind quickly, and I grappled with the uncertainty of whether this was merely my imagination or a genuine spiritual encounter. The overwhelming presence I felt was nonthreatening and feminine in nature.

Driven by curiosity, I reached for the recorder and initiated playback, eager to confirm or debunk the sensations I was experiencing before sharing them with my roommate. To our astonishment, within moments of the recording, an unidentifiable female voice—echoing the same voice my roommate had attested to hearing before through her experiences—let out a heavy sigh, followed by an unintelligible whisper. The woman's speech carried a mysterious accent, one that remained elusive in its origin.

While it may not have met the criteria for a Class A EVP (electronic voice phenomena), which denotes the highest quality and clearest evidence in paranormal research, it undeniably held significance. It was a subtle but undeniable glimpse into the enigmatic world of the supernatural, leaving us with more questions than answers.

That same week, I had a strange encounter with our neighbor, who occupied one half of the house, but whom I had never seen before. I was getting out of my car in the parking lot, returning late one night from an event I had attended, when I saw her emerging from her side of the house. Given that I had never heard any activity emanating from that side of the house and had never laid eyes on her before, her very existence remained shrouded in mystery. Even the property owner had no knowledge of her occupation or daily activities, rendering her a total enigma. That night, I had a chance meeting with her, though the meeting was brief, lasting only a few moments. The encounter would change the way I would think about the paranormal activity that was going on in the house.

The only connection I had was through the wall in my closet. It was the only portion of the house that was shared between the two apartments, though I never heard a sound coming from her side of the house. The night I saw this mysterious woman walking through the parking lot, facing the creek that looped around to the back of the house. She only said one word to me, a simple "hello," before she got into her car to drive off. As insignificant as the meeting was, it was her attire and a sudden realization that changed things and opened a new world that I knew existed but never delved into myself.

She was dressed in a long black cloak with the hood pulled up over her head, revealing only a small hint of red hair against the soft black velvet that framed her face. Her thick black glasses concealed her eyes, but a pentagram dangled from her neck. It was clear that she was dressed for a mid-summer's eve ritual somewhere in the shadows of Nashville. At the time, I didn't think much about this incident. However, the events that unfolded later that same week emphasized the idea that she might have sensed the energy in the house in some way, and I somehow understood that she was aware of the activity, possibly even drawing it towards herself. This was something I would later learn to be relatively easy to do.

It was Midsummer's solstice, also known as St. John's Eve, an ancient holiday once recognized by the Roman Catholic Church, the Anglican Church, and the Church of England, as well as being one of the largest celebrations in voodoo culture. These festivities commemorate the shortest night of the year and originated in the fourth century to honor the birth of St. John the Baptist, who is believed to have been born six months before the birth of Christ. This holds significance as John the Baptist was seen as "preparing the way for Jesus."

In medieval popular belief, St. John's Eve was imbued with special power, but it was also a time when evil forces were thought to be active. To ward off these malevolent forces, bonfires were traditionally lit. In a sense, I couldn't help but feel that my connection with this neighbor might be opening a gateway for me to enter the spirit world—a realm that had previously been closed and forgotten.

What I knew about the holiday was that the New Orleans version of the holiday stretched back to the 1830s when the renowned Voodoo priestess Marie Laveau began hosting annual feasts on the banks of Lake Pontchartrain. The memory of the Haitian revolution was still vivid in people's minds during that time. Popular loas, such as Brigid, the Archangel Michael, and St. John the Baptist himself, became the entities invoked to open gateways for spirit contact, connections to ancestors, spiritual supplications, and favors. They were also the central focal points of Midsummer's Eve.

My neighbor was undoubtedly discreetly heading to such a celebration. There wasn't anything unusual about this, except that at that time, particularly in the deep South, it was rare to meet anyone who practiced a religion or faith other than Southern Baptist. Anything other than Christianity was considered heathenism by the general culture, and I fully understood why she would want to keep her attire under wraps. I did not follow the Southern Baptist beliefs at the time, but I was aware of how prominent they were, especially to those they considered outsiders. Keep in mind, this was a time when they were still asking what church you were affiliated with in most job and school related applications and wine sales were considered the devil's juice.

Something strange occurred a few mornings after I met my neighbor. I was returning home from an overnight trip when I saw an ambulance parked outside our house, surrounded by emergency personnel. They were there to collect the remains of my neighbor, who had suddenly passed away from a stroke in the early hours of that morning. My roommate, myself, and the property owner were questioned about whether we knew of any friends or relatives she may have had who visited her, but we couldn't provide any information. Later that week, as no known relatives came forward to claim her belongings, the property owner hired a junk removal company to clear out her possessions from the house. A mound of her things was tossed into a large trash receptacle in the parking lot. In just a few short days, everything that defined a person's existence was gathered up and discarded into a trash bin, destined for a dump.

I came to believe that my neighbor had something to do with the paranormal activity in the house, but I couldn't put my finger on it. I kept dreaming of her opening a gateway to the Spirit world in the house, only to realize that this gateway she opened was for me to explore.

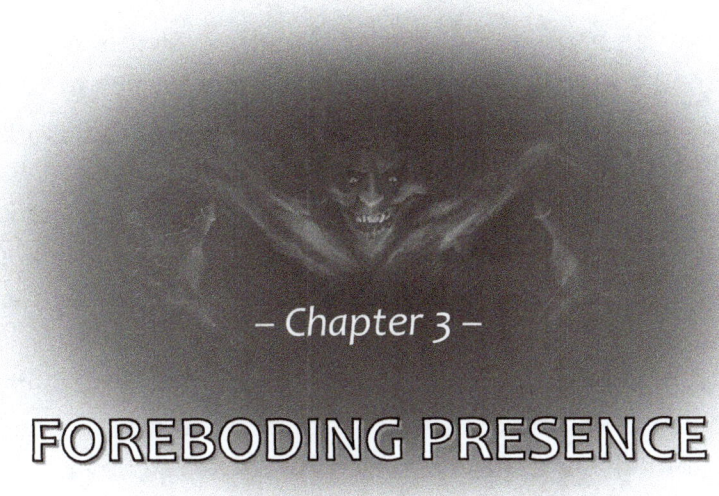

– Chapter 3 –

FOREBODING PRESENCE

"There are those who believe that evil spirits can imbue mud and straw with life, breathing wretched souls into inanimate objects to create living beings, and that dybbuks walk among us, leading us to temptation and ruin."
– Alice Hoffman

Strange phenomena began to manifest, not only within myself but also in the vicinity of the house. One late night, as I pulled into the driveway of the parking lot, my car's headlights revealed a shadowy, shrouded figure standing about four feet tall beside a tree, hovering over the creek. The figure appeared to resemble a small human, draped in some kind of cloak that covered its head, shoulders, and body. For the brief seconds I beheld this figure, it seemed almost transparent, allowing my car's light to pass through it. My heart sank, and I leaped out of my car, sprinting into the house, turning on every light along the way.

The property owner hired various people to work on the

adjoining apartment. These included a cleaning crew, a handyman to work on repairs, and a new carpet installer to get the place fixed up for new tenants. They came in and out during the day, but the place remained empty and locked after four in the afternoons. The trash receptacle remained outside so that the handyman could toss in the odd cabinets, adding to all that was left of our mysterious neighbor's life.

I began to hear strange noises coming from the wall in the closet late at night. At first, I thought it was just my imagination, spooked by the shrouded shadow I had seen earlier, but my roommate heard them too. They started as mere scratching sounds on the walls. My cat would often stare at the walls, as if sensing something amiss. It sounded like a rodent was inside the wall. I informed the property owner that I suspected rodents, and he hired an exterminator to set traps. After a week, the traps remained empty, and the landlord dismissed it as the house settling due to humidity. However, the noises persisted.

Our house shared the parking lot with another house on the property, constructed around the same time and in the same architectural style as ours. An older woman lived in this house alone. I had seen her going to and from her car, but I had never personally spoken to her as she kept to herself. She, too, never had visitors and seemed to be a loner. Within just a few weeks of our neighbor's passing, something tragic would occur to this other neighbor.

She was known to go out late at night and return in the early morning hours. On one of these early morning ventures, she tragically stumbled to her death backward down a flight of stairs. She was discovered by one of the people working in the apartment adjacent to ours the next morning. It was a rare and unbelievable event – two immediate neighbors passing suddenly on the same property! Similarly, she, too, had no family or loved ones. I do not know what the conversation was between the property owners, or if there was any conversation at all. I only know that these strange events seemed to complement one another, adding to the paranormal activity that was picking up around us.

Another large trash bin appeared outside in the front of the house, ready to collect the belongings of yet another life. Our parking lot became something of a dumpster diver's dream. Later, I learned from the property owner of her house that this lady had an alcohol addiction that was attributed to her accident. However, the strange thing that stood out to me was that both women did not have family and loved ones. They were isolated and alone. I couldn't help but think that all these coincidences related to the paranormal haunting. It was almost as if whatever spirit was haunting the grounds was picking out people who were isolated. Or was it isolating these people? I couldn't help but ponder about how my own relationship unraveled in just a few weeks of moving onto the property, without any previous indicators that something was wrong.

In the wake of the unfortunate demise of these two women, the once-subtle paranormal occurrences within the house took a chilling and ominous turn. A heaviness lingered over me, and over the house itself. One late evening, I walked into my closet to change and heard a low, rumbling, disembodied growl from the corner of my closet, where I found a small wooden crucifix tucked beneath the shelf. With chills running down my spine, I reached for the shelf where I kept a pair of boots and pulled the small wooden crucifix out, holding it in disbelief in my hand. I was fully convinced that the cross had been placed in that spot by the previous tenants. With my hair standing on end, I just wanted to run.

Besides the eerie visual and auditory paranormal occurrences that haunted me, it seemed as though the malevolent presence had a sinister grasp on my mind, unleashing a relentless assault that began with a series of chilling nightmares. These recurring night terrors featured a haunting figure clad in a hooded shroud, the very same entity I had previously glimpsed lurking near the creek. While tales of sleep paralysis often involve encounters with a female specter known as the "hag," my ordeal diverged from the norm. Instead, I found myself trapped in the clutches of an enigmatic, genderless, dark-cloaked apparition. In each harrowing incident, I remained aware that I was ensnared within a dream, yet I remained powerless to rouse myself from the nightmarish clutches of the spectral tormentor.

Each time these occurrences happened, I could not breathe, move, or even scream for help. All I could do was look up at the ceiling, past the faceless entity, and mentally call out for help from Archangel Michael. Archangel Michael is often regarded as a protector of people spiritually in various religious and spiritual traditions, though I did not know at the time that this presence could help. The first time I was attacked by this shrouded figure, not knowing what else to do, I felt compelled to call on this angel. In response, the entity screamed back in my face, releasing me as it swept back up into the ceiling. The initial experience left me feeling scared and vulnerable, marking the first time I had ever feared the paranormal.

The "hag" nightmares had me on edge as I continued my daily routine, trying to forget what was happening. I had not told my roommate about the dream because I feared it would intensify the situation. Paranormal phenomena began to happen more frequently, and she was getting uneasy with the activity. She began searching for a paranormal investigation group that could possibly give us some advice, but there just weren't a lot of people talking about the paranormal.

There was no longer a specific time of day when the paranormal activity occurred, as it had during the earlier phases of the hunting. It seemed to happen at all hours, with no discernible correlation or pattern.

One Saturday afternoon, my roommate was in the kitchen, cooking, while I was tidying up my room. As I walked into the closet to grab a vacuum, the room suddenly felt heavy and crowded, as though I were surrounded by unseen presences. With the vacuum in my hand, I turned back into my bedroom and approached the double French doors to open the curtains. Bright sunlight filtered in, but the room appeared hazy. Suddenly, I spotted a figure moving from the middle of the room into the bathroom I had just vacated.

Startled, I dropped the vacuum's handle and swiftly turned around, initially thinking it might be my roommate, but to my surprise, there was no one there. The figure I had just witnessed was translucent enough for me to see the doorway through it, and it bore a striking resemblance to a young boy. He was dressed in a gray military Civil War coat, with a hat pulled low over the front of his face. This apparition appeared to be around four feet tall.

Out of everything that was happening, there was one incident that changed me in such a profound way that it seemed to spiritually awaken me. I was alone in my room late in the evening. My roommate was away for the weekend, leaving me by myself for a rare Friday night. By this point, it wasn't unusual to witness shadows darting along the walls or through the long hallway. However, these occurrences were always easily dismissed as the mind playing tricks. The hallway, in particular, bore the brunt of the traffic throughout the house.

The apartment next door had remained vacant for several weeks, yet I continued to hear unintelligible voices and tapping against the wall during the late hours of the night. Strangely, the more I strained to decipher what the voices were saying, the more distorted they became. In the beginning, I dismissed these phenomena, attributing them to the possibility of workers tending to the neighboring apartment. However, an unsettling realization eventually dawned upon me, one that I couldn't easily ignore.

These eerie occurrences related to the apartment next door were strictly nocturnal, always transpiring in the middle of the night, hours after the empty apartment had been locked up. No matter how hard I tried, I couldn't find a simple explanation for these unsettling sounds. It became increasingly clear that the activity emanating from that closet was far from anything normal.

On a particularly active night, I was jolted awake by the persistent sound of knocking, as if someone were rapping on the wall. Unable to return to sleep, I hastily inserted earplugs into my ears and reached for the book I had been reading, determined to ignore the paranormal disturbances and find some respite. There were countless nights I had spent engrossed in a book, reading well into the early hours. My Burmese cat nestled beside me on the bed, offering silent companionship. The only source of light in the house emanated from an antique oil lamp I had repurposed into an electric lamp on the nightstand.

In the dim illumination, I was abruptly startled by the manifestation of another four-foot entity right next to my bed. While I was engrossed in the book's pages, I sensed its presence moving from the corner of my eye. What struck me as particularly eerie about this shadow was the way it moved – it seemed to be swiftly swept downward, disappearing under the bed. There was no lateral movement; it simply descended in an unnatural, unhuman-like manner.

The shadow materialized abruptly, towering over me. In a matter of mere seconds, it swiftly descended, appearing to vanish into the floor. The presence of this shadow triggered a tumultuous cascade of emotions within me – terror, shock, and a profound sense of powerlessness. It disrupted my overall sense of well-being within the house.

Once I had managed to regain my composure following that unsettling incident, I made it a habit to keep the lamp on when I went to sleep from that night forward. However, on that very night, a similar occurrence happened. I was roused from my slumber by what sounded like knocking, emanating once again from my closet. Still reeling from the earlier encounter with the mysterious shadow, I was filled with trepidation about venturing into the closet to investigate.

I attempted to dismiss the strange knocking and return to sleep, but as often happens in such situations, an eerie presence hung heavily in the room. I couldn't resist the urge to glance in the direction of the doorway leading into the bathroom and walk-in closet. Just as I did, I witnessed a tall figure, adorned with what appeared to be a hat, glide swiftly across the door frame. It was accompanied by a deep and unmistakable voice—a man's voice that whispered with an eerie harshness, "get out." It was the notorious Hat Man entity that so many claim to have encountered.

Already deeply shaken by the unsettling noises and the enigmatic shadow I had witnessed earlier in the night, fear gripped me. I quickly dressed, left my residence, and sought refuge in a 24-hour coffee shop on Elliston Place in West Nashville, where I hoped to regain my composure. Ironically, next to this coffee house, there stood a small occult store, though it was closed at the time. The sight of this shop triggered memories of another establishment in South Nashville owned by a renowned Nashville-based practicing witch and psychic medium. That very night, fueled by my need for answers and solace, I inquired around to find the location of her shop.

The recent surge in paranormal activity, coupled with the tragic deaths of my neighbors, cast a heavy shadow over me in the days that followed. I couldn't help but wonder if the intensifying energy in the house was somehow fueled by these grim events. In my relentless quest for answers, I delved deep into paranormal research, discovering a prevailing belief that negative entities, particularly demonic ones, are drawn to specific social and economic circumstances affecting those they afflict.

These circumstances often include poverty, dysfunctional family dynamics, and addiction. Both of my deceased neighbors had lived isolated lives, estranged from their families, and one of them had battled alcoholism, which ultimately led to her premature demise. These eerie parallels extended into my own life, as I, too, found myself estranged from my family. It left me pondering a disquieting question: Could these malevolent entities somehow sense these shared aspects of our lives?

– Chapter 4 –

AN AWAKENING

"The first time I called myself a 'Witch' was the most magical moment of my life."
— Margot Adler."

Having tracked down the mystical emporium belonging to the enigmatic psychic medium and self-proclaimed witch, I stood before a quaint 1940s cottage nestled discreetly behind the renowned Sam & Zoe's coffee haven in the heart of Berry Hill, Nashville. The area was a run-down residential district undergoing a revitalization effort to rezone and remodel the 1940s houses into music recording studios, artisan shops, eateries, and favorite musician hangout spots like my personal favorite, the House of Blues Studio. Berry Hill predominantly took shape during World War II, occupying the grounds of Elmwood, a former antebellum cotton plantation owned by a prominent Nashville historical figure, William Wells Berry.

It was the first community in Davidson County to become incorporated, and even has its own police station.

This locale brims with folklore and tales linked to the Civil War, entwined with somber events from its history. Remarkably, it's also home to the city's oldest burial ground, Woodlawn Cemetery, where the slumbering souls rest in eternal repose.

In keeping with the charming ambiance of Berry Hill, the metaphysical shop had no designated parking area. A single narrow driveway, reserved for the shop owner, was all that existed, while street parking proved to be a challenging endeavor. My salvation came in the form of an empty space across the street, conveniently situated just outside Sam & Zoe's coffee shop.

Amidst the neighborhood's quaint wood-siding and clapboard cottages, the shop known as "Goddess & the Moon" emerged as a striking outlier. Stepping across the street toward the radiant yellow abode, its sign skillfully painted above the overhang of the front porch, I found myself instantly captivated by the yard's assortment of eccentric art and its unique exterior decor. As I entered the house, a warm welcome awaited me in the form of an African Grey parrot, later introduced as "Cherokee," perched elegantly by the expansive front window, fixating its gaze outward onto the enchanting yard.

Meeting Tish for the first time enveloped me in a profound sense of awe and déjà vu. It wasn't her physical presence that I recalled so vividly but rather the aura that surrounded her. In an instant, memories of my childhood experiences with the paranormal flooded back, rendering me momentarily speechless and unsure how to broach the topic of supernatural occurrences in my home. The shop exuded an aura of peculiarity and eclecticism, and yet, an inexplicable sense of familiarity washed over me. The mystical embellishments, replete with spiritual elements, angels, and enigmatic potions, served as a poignant reminder of the magical tapestry woven through my life, interwoven with countless paranormal encounters. In a curious twist, it almost seemed as if this place held the potential to steer me toward an alternate life path, one I had always been destined to traverse.

Upon my first encounter with Tish, I must confess, I found myself at a loss for words and questions. Nervousness gripped me, not solely because I had never met a self-proclaimed witch, but also due to the tumultuous memories resurfacing from my past. As if in response to my disquiet, the parrot perched nearby emitted a cackle before cordially greeting me. Amused yet unsettled by the bird's penetrating gaze, I stood rooted in the doorway, momentarily tongue-tied. Seated before a computer nestled in the corner of the main room, Tish reassured me that Cherokee posed no threat and extended a welcoming invitation into her enchanting shop.

The walls came alive with vibrant shades of orange, yellow, and green, their brilliance accentuated by a gilded shimmer as sunlight streamed through the expansive front window. Along one wall, a shelf stretched the entire length, adorned with a collection of gem-filled bowls and radiant crystals. On the opposite side, Gothic-style robes and brightly colored tunics hung gracefully from hangers. Dominating the center of the room, an assortment of tables of varying heights proudly displayed cast iron cauldrons, boxes adorned with pagan symbols, and an array of candles and incense. While Tish continued to type away at her computer in the corner, her watchful gaze remained palpable, leaving me acutely aware of her scrutiny.

"What brings you in today?" she inquired, her fingers dancing noisily across the keyboard. It was a straightforward question, yet it left me feeling oddly exposed. My mind raced, attempting to craft a response that would only hint at my true purpose for being there, but words eluded me, and I found myself struggling to conjure an answer.

"Just browsing," I finally replied, trying to maintain an air of casual curiosity, masking any hint of my inexperience in the world of charcoal, pentagrams, and witches. Tish, her attention still absorbed by the computer screen, continued typing, occasionally sweeping a stray blonde lock from her eyes. Her vibrant dress harmonized with the kaleidoscopic walls, adorned with swirls, stars, and bright blue fabric. In hushed tones, I went ahead with my exploration, briefly perusing a book from the shelf before gently returning it to its place. Everything within the shop was undeniably captivating! Summoning my courage, I eventually found my voice and began to pose the questions that had been swirling within me.

"Do you offer readings?" I blurted out suddenly, my gaze drawn to a small sign beside the cash register that listed prices for various magical services.

"Yes," she replied, her gaze shifting away from the computer, as though she had predicted my precise inquiry. "Would you like a reading? I have a client scheduled in forty minutes, so I can make time for you right now."

While I didn't necessarily seek a reading, my true desire was to engage in a one-on-one conversation with her, and somehow, I had the impression that she had picked up on this. Tish rose from her office chair, gracefully moving past me and proceeding down a lengthy corridor that materialized from a towering false wall nearly twelve feet high. This wall cleverly partitioned the space, forming two rooms accessible via the corridor, each adorned with vibrant wall tapestries.

Tish parted the curtain to the first room and ushered me

into a cozy lounge area that seemed as though it had been designed for a deity. A sumptuous high-backed golden chair occupied the center of the room, positioned before an intricately carved round table draped with a luxurious deep purple velvet cloth. I was guided to take a seat in a simple, plush chair placed opposite her ornate "witch's" throne.

A high-pitched squeal from Cherokee echoed from the front of the house, the sound carrying effortlessly through the open rooms, courtesy of the vaulted ceilings that graced the remodeled interior. The walls, adorned with colorful lithographs and paintings, formed harmonious symphonies of art, leaving no bare inch untouched. Splashes of golden paint sparkled between the frames and fabrics, adding an enchanting touch. Positioned on the wall furthest from where I sat, opposite the hallway, a bookcase groaned under the weight of books on witchcraft, art, and goddesses. Precious crystal rocks, an array of colors, adorned the ledges of each shelf, nestled snugly within crevices wherever they found space.

Tish settled into her goddess chair across from me, her gaze resting on me over a crystal ball and a deck of well-worn tarot cards. Placing one hand gently over the oversized deck, she closed her eyes, taking a deep, deliberate breath—a practice I would come to adopt and carry with me for years to come. Then, she leaned back in her chair, and for a few moments, we sat in reverent silence as she slipped into the realm of Spirit, a meditative state or trance to quiet the mind and connect with the spirit realm. The term Spirit here refers to the collective spirit realm.

"What brings you in today?" she inquired, setting in motion a conversation that would rekindle my curiosity and start my journey into mediumship and the spiritual realm I had once known but had momentarily set aside during my college years. As we delved into discussions about the spirit world and my early experiences with it, we then moved into the peculiar occurrences within my rental house, our conversation meandered into the realm of more personal current events. The reading extended far beyond the typical duration she allotted to clients, but this was a unique case. Her next appointment was twenty minutes late, and she had yet another fifteen-minute wait ahead of her.

While the exact words of our conversation have faded into the mists of time and distance, several key insights from that encounter would profoundly shape my perspective on the paranormal world. I hadn't anticipated anyone believing the extraordinary events my roommate and I had experienced, but to my surprise, she absorbed every detail with genuine understanding. Instead of charging me for my time, she extended an invitation to return, encouraging more sessions of what she endearingly referred to as "witch talk."

As I shared stories of my early childhood and the series of paranormal encounters that had punctuated my life, comparing them to the happenings within the house, she drew a fascinating conclusion. According to her, I possessed latent abilities that begged to be acknowledged and nurtured. It was a revelation that would set me on a transformative path of self-discovery and spiritual growth.

When I initially entered the shop, a sense of powerlessness gripped me. Yet, in the company of Tish, I was outfitted with courage and a newfound sense of empowerment, gradually realizing that my spiritual influence ran deeper than I had ever imagined. I was entrusted with the profound task of uncovering my true spiritual self, armed with a list of books to immerse myself in, delving into the realms of spirit communication and meditation.

One of the most pivotal takeaways from our

conversation was the idea that individuals with abilities, like me, could inadvertently draw spirits towards them, akin to moths drawn to a light source. Tish's theory was that the negative energy in the house might have been magnetically drawn to me. It was a concept that would reverberate not only throughout the haunting of that home but for many years to come. We attract energies in accordance with the vibrations we emit, governed by the laws of attraction.

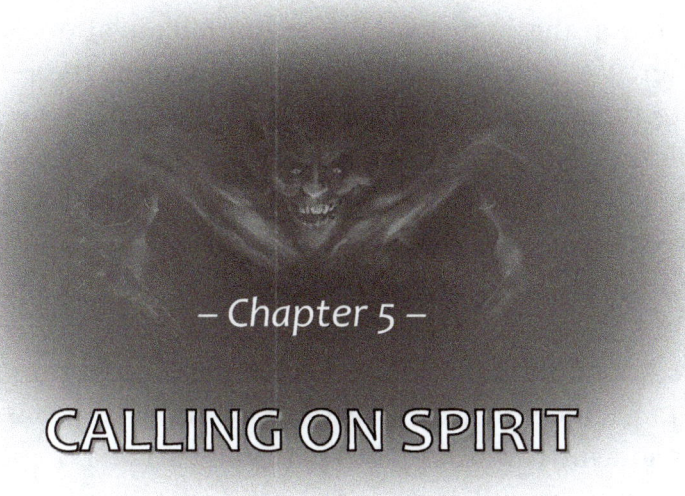

– Chapter 5 –

CALLING ON SPIRIT

**"To realize that you are not your thoughts is when you
begin to awaken spiritually."
— Eckhart Tolle**

The indelible mark left by Hurricane Katrina's devastating rampage through New Orleans in 2005 remains etched in the memories of those who bore witness to its fury. This catastrophic event stands as one of the most destructive natural disasters in the annals of the United States.

Katrina, accompanied by its catastrophic flooding, inflicted extensive damage and displacement, casting countless residents into a tumultuous battle for survival and the daunting task of rebuilding their lives. Although I was not personally affected by this catastrophic storm, I had the opportunity to report on the aftermath, witnessing the harrowing aftermath as the floodwaters gradually receded.

The enduring narrative of the hurricane's aftermath continues to hold a profound place in my life. It serves as a poignant reminder of the tumultuous chaos and widespread devastation that unfolded in the immediate aftermath of the disaster. Yet, it also stands as a testament to the remarkable resilience and unwavering hope that gradually rose from the rubble.

A few weeks after the storm's fury had subsided, I received an invitation to collaborate with FEMA, joining their efforts to chronicle the lives of those engaged in the arduous cleanup process. Armed with an undergraduate degree in communications and having started on a master's program in journalism, I recognized that the job would not be financially rewarding, but it would provide the invaluable experiential foundation I sought for a career change. It granted me the unique opportunity to bear witness to the unwavering resolve of individuals who had opted to remain and confront the tempest, offering a profound testament to the resilience of the human spirit, even in the most trying of circumstances.

The cleanup process unfolded at a painstakingly slow and grueling pace, as the city wrestled with the colossal devastation wrought by the hurricane and the ensuing deluge. A significant portion of the city still languished in darkness, and the remnants of debris and wreckage littered the streetscape. Though the floodwaters had retreated, New Orleans was confronted with an enormous cleanup endeavor that would demand years of tireless effort to be fully realized.

Dedicated volunteers and tireless emergency workers labored relentlessly to clear the streets, eliminate debris, and reinstate vital services like electricity and water. Numerous sections of the city remained uninhabitable, bearing the scars of homes and businesses severely battered or obliterated. The city's celebrated music and cultural havens, too, bore the brunt, as many venues and landmarks suffered considerable damage.

Yet, amid the wreckage, a profound sense of resilience and resolve emanated from the residents I encountered. Communities rallied together, offering unwavering support, and an influx of volunteers from all corners of the country descended upon the city, extending a helping hand to aid in the recovery. It was an era of profound hardship for New Orleans, but it also shone as a testament to the extraordinary strength and tenacity exhibited in the face of insurmountable adversity.

Late September in New Orleans maintained its characteristic humidity, even by the city's standards. Armed with camera gear, I checked into the historic Hotel Baronne Plaza, nestled in the Lower Central Business District—an area steeped in the rich tapestry of New Orleans' history. Erected in 1931, the hotel retained its original granite façade and showcased Art Deco stone architecture. The lobby radiates elegance, graced by the presence of stained-glass skylights, regal columns, and floors fashioned from genuine marble. In those trying times, it stood as one of the few functioning hotels in the city that hadn't been completely commandeered by locals, first responders, and FEMA workers. The hotel's garage held onto several feet of debris and mud, vestiges of the flooding waters. I had no alternative but to leave my car parked several blocks away in an empty casino lot, praying that it would escape any unwanted attention. With a Pelican case laden with camera equipment in tow, I set out on a solitary walk down the desolate stretch of Canal Street—an experience I realized would probably never be reenacted, with not a soul in sight. The city streets were dark, quiet, and void of tourists, who would have flooded this side of Canal Street before the storm.

New Orleans was an eerie and unsettling place to be.

Despite the emptiness of the streets, a palpable sense of dark energy enveloped the city, making it feel suffocating and oppressive. Ghosts seemed to lurk behind every mound of trash. The city smelled terribly from flooded sewage, trash and even decomposing bodies in some cases. Block by block, teams of people would clean out the houses and get them ready to be bulldozed.

During those few weeks, I took pictures of numerous individuals and conducted interviews of volunteers, FEMA workers, and distraught homeowners who were attempting to salvage whatever they could. They meticulously combed through each house, sorting appliances, trash, and bags into separate piles, and gathering hazardous materials for safe disposal. In addition to the hazardous materials, they also had to collect decomposing bodies, which were still being discovered in some of the homes. It was the first time for me to encounter the smell of a decomposing corpse, and it's something I can never forget. The combination of the sour smell of decomposition gases, and the sweet and musty odor of decayed and bloated flesh was acrid and nauseating, and it lingered everywhere in the air.

During one of my journeys into the flood-ravaged regions, I encountered a unique and life-altering experience. I struck up a spontaneous conversation with a stranger, and to my surprise, it evolved into a profound discussion about the spirit world. This serendipitous encounter challenged my preconceived notions and considerably expanded my understanding of the supernatural realm. I had already come to realize that the spirit world was not merely an abstract concept but a palpable force that could be perceived and met in various ways. Furthermore, thanks to my discussions with Tish, I had begun to entertain the idea that we might attract negative energy into our lives. However, I had not yet embraced the belief that we could intentionally summon entities from the spirit world.

This newfound discovery ignited within me a heightened sense of curiosity and wonder about the enigmas of the universe. It also deepened my appreciation for the profound power of human connection when it came to exploring these mysteries.

Calling upon spirits is an ancient practice rooted in the quest for guidance, solace, or safeguarding from a higher power or energy that transcends the physical realm. It is an act of vulnerability, an invitation to the cosmos to intervene, and offer insight, sagacity, or fortitude. However, what occurs when that call is heeded, and the spirit manifests in manners that push the boundaries of our convictions and comprehension of the world? Can this somehow backfire on the person conjuring up a Spirit?

The notion of a spirit responding to my summons was simultaneously breathtaking and disconcerting, filling me with a sense of marvel and an enhanced reverence for the enigmatic influences that mold my existence. My fascination with the spirit world was already fervent, and I yearned to explore what might occur if I delved even deeper into it. By a twist of fate, I stumbled upon this novel concept firsthand through an encounter with an elderly man in New Orleans.

In one of the neighborhoods being primed for teardown, I met a man inscribing sigils on the side of his home. In disbelief, I watched for a moment as he drew on the vintage asbestos siding, of what I presumed to be his home, while humming. He appeared to be deep in meditation. This would be my first real encounter with voodoo culture, something you will not truly find today in the French Quarters of New Orleans. While there is some truth to Maria Laveau's Voodoo Shop and the Voodoo Museum, those who are real practitioners would have no need to shop in these places. Nor would a true practitioner be a tourist spectacle on Bourbon Street. Instead, those who truly practice this religion are hidden from prying eyes. Had I been a tourist, I doubt this man would have conversed with me at all.

The shotgun-style house he inhabited bore the familiar crimson "X" mark, conspicuously spray-painted, a symbol shared by many other dwellings along the same block. I watched for a while as the man, clad in worn jeans and a grime-covered t-shirt, etched peculiar symbols onto the side of his house using a piece of chalk. He seemed to be attempting to establish contact with the spirits he had served within this residence before the storm, invoking them to accompany him to his new abode in Hammond, Louisiana.

Our exchange unfolded swiftly on the street in front of his residence. The elderly man, his speech adorned with a rich Creole accent, seemed rather disinterested in our conversation, likely due to my camera equipment. However, he did begrudgingly share some perspective on his unusual undertaking.

He imparted a fascinating perspective during our conversation, challenging the prevailing notion in contemporary paranormal thought that spirits could be trapped in a particular location. According to his viewpoint, spirits possessed free will, and they couldn't be controlled like one might command a dog. Instead, he subscribed to the belief that you could summon spirit entities to intervene on your behalf or awaken them to a different reality, as he was attempting to do in this instance. Essentially, he sought to rouse the spirits of his ancestors, whom he believed he had served in this house, with the hope that they would accompany him to his new place.

While the concept of omnipresence is a topic for another

chapter, it stands to reason those spirits, unencumbered by physical boundaries or the constraints of time and space, would possess the freedom to move from one place to another at their own volition.

This idea of summoning spiritual entities, such as angels, for guidance had always seemed intimidating to me, given my inherent sense of insignificance in comparison to these divine beings. However, the concept of reaching out to the spirit realm resonated with me on a profound level. I gradually came to understand that the size of my physical form or the constraints of my human existence did not limit my ability to connect with the spiritual realm. Rather, it was my willingness to open myself to the possibility of their presence and my belief in their willingness to aid me on my spiritual journey that held true significance. This realization allowed me to cast aside my self-doubt and wholeheartedly embrace the notion of seeking spiritual guidance whenever the need arose. It marked a transformative shift in my perspective, granting me the courage to explore the boundless realms of the spiritual universe.

I mulled over the perplexing events that had been unfolding in my haunted home back in Nashville, particularly concerning my late neighbor, whom I witnessed going to a St. John's Eve ceremony months ago. Had she summoned a spirit with malicious intent toward her, triggering her ultimate demise? I was beginning to learn that in certain spiritual traditions, one's intentions and energy can attract spirits or entities that resonate with them. Consequently, if someone is intentionally or inadvertently invoking negative entities, it can lead to adverse consequences. Those who unwittingly invite negative energies into their lives may experience harmful effects. The thought crossed my mind that maybe my own curiosity and experimentation were inadvertently opening doors into the unknown, potentially drawing in forces that I hadn't fully comprehended. All around me, the spirit world was opening more and more.

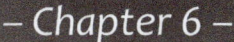

– Chapter 6 –

PIERCING THE DARKNESS

"When you look ahead and darkness is all you see, faith and determination will pull you through."
— Drake

Every time I returned home from being out of town, I was greeted with fresh accounts of inexplicable events from my roommate. As the activity became more violent, she sought help from a paranormal investigative team. By then, we had collected enough EVPs on my digital recorder to convince a paranormal investigative team from the Nashville area to conduct a formal investigation. The team of paranormal investigators used my room as a base to document and analyze the extent of the disturbances over a weekend stay at our house while I was away. The investigators believed it would be wise for me to stay away from the premises during their investigation since I appeared to be at the center of the paranormal activity.

When they arrived, they spent an entire Friday night setting up equipment, taking baseline readings with an EMF reader and interviewing my neighbor. They stayed in my room overnight for two nights, collecting data, and experiencing everything from the subtle shuffling sound I would so often hear at night from movement of a fantom entity, and their experiences left me completely astonished after they did their reveal.

The team consisted of five individuals who were fans of the popular television show *Ghost Hunters*. They adopted a similar approach to their investigations, meaning they didn't believe in having a medium present. They felt that this would unduly influence the direction of the investigation. Instead, they had a technical person equipped with cameras, walkie-talkies, EMF detectors, digital recorders, a historian, two investigators, and a lead investigator who was a member of a national paranormal research association. Despite being a relatively new team, they had already conducted several investigations in and around the Nashville area, including one at the infamous Governor's Mansion.

The Governor's Mansion is an impressive and historic building that has served as the official residence of the governor of Tennessee since 1949. Situated on a 10-acre plot in the Oak Hill neighborhood of Nashville, this mansion was constructed in the 1920s and boasts a neoclassical design with a grand portico, Ionic columns, and a striking entrance hall. Visitors can explore its formal rooms, including a drawing room, library, and dining room, all elegantly furnished and adorned with artwork from Tennessee artists.

Over the years, the mansion has hosted countless events and dignitaries, ranging from governors and lawmakers to celebrities and foreign leaders. Furthermore, it is open to the public for guided tours, offering visitors a glimpse into the rich history and culture of Tennessee. However, despite its stately appearance and prestigious history, the Governor's

Mansion has not been immune to rumors of paranormal activity. Some visitors and staff report strange sounds and sightings of ghostly figures, fueling speculation that the mansion may indeed be haunted. Whether or not these reports hold any truth, they only add to the mystique and allure of this remarkable Tennessee landmark. Interestingly, this mansion is not far from our own house.

Our house turned out to be the paranormal group's first case with solid evidence of paranormal activity, and they were both excited and deeply concerned about the nature of the haunting. They conducted their investigation without the modern-day flashy high-tech SLR cameras, LIDAR mapping equipment, or even a ghost box, a device that has become commonplace for paranormal enthusiasts today. Surprisingly, looking back at the events, the absence of expensive equipment seemed to have lent authenticity to their reported findings in that they were genuinely interested in the case, me and my roommate and seemed less concerned with collecting evidence to showcase themselves. They also appeared to be more attuned to the activity. All too often, I see investigators today spending most of their focus on the technological aspects of their investigations, with their eyes glued to a cell phone application or some other equipment rather than paying attention to the activity happening right in front of them.

Using only a small Sony stationary camera in my room, they captured one of the most compelling pieces of evidence that I ever witnessed from a small paranormal team not featured on television. A four-foot shadow manifested in the doorway to my bathroom and disappeared into the wall. It looked as if it materialized right out of the side of the floor. It very much resembled what I had seen at the foot of my bed on several occasions and what my roommate had seen in the hallway. The entirety of the shadow on film lasted just seconds and had to be slowed down to view. Around the same time that this evidence was captured, the team had caught several EVPs from different disembodied voices in the room.

Most of the disembodied voices captured with their digital recorders were not heard by the investigators that night. It refers to the supposed appearance of voices or sounds that are believed to be of paranormal origin, which is captured on electronic recording devices such as audio recorders or radio equipment and is often associated with attempts to communicate with spirits or ghosts.

What astonished the investigators was the numerous voices they heard. The captured voices comprised two young children, a gruff-sounding man, and a woman, along with growling sounds, shuffling, and tapping. Many of them were considered class A EVPs by the investigators, which means they could be heard clearly from the recording and did not sound like whispers. To qualify as a class A EVP, the voice or sound must be audible and easily understandable without any enhancement or amplification.

In this case, the investigators did not edit the recordings at all. One of the voices asked several times throughout the night, "Where's Crystal?" in a small child's voice. My favorite EVP of all time was recorded during their investigation. A male responded to one of the investigators who called out to the spirits that the team was leaving and that this would be their last chance to speak. The direct response was from a male's deep voice, "Don't come back." The leading concern for the investigators was the multitude of voices coming through, as if my bedroom was some sort of vortex. Were these all-different human spirits, or was it a negative entity, such as a demonic presence, mimicking these voices?

The lead investigator, Janet, was an older woman, well into her retirement years, who claimed to be a psychic medium and paranormal investigator for over twenty years. She had a somewhat cranky demeanor and was quite stoic about how things should be done. She came to meet me, accompanied by a historian who was also part of the team. One late evening, we all gathered around my kitchen table to discuss what transpired during the investigation and to hear the lead investigator's recommendations. Uncharacteristically for the general Southern custom of spending the first ten minutes of any meeting in chitchat, she got right down to business.

Janet began her discourse by stating that she felt as though the energy was always present in the land but that the energy was being drawn out and intensified by the combination of someone initially opening a portal (perhaps the woman who died in the duplex next to us) and by myself for having abilities and giving the entity attention. This information was confirmation of what I had been thinking. This history of the property being directly on the front line for the battle of Nashville always harbored a sense of awe and reverence for the soldiers who had fought and died so long ago, and the legacy they had left behind for me.

In my personal collection of growing haunted objects, I keep a jar containing Civil War artifacts I found around the property. These include three-ringer lead bullets, part of a bayonet, and even a four-pounder cannon shot, along with cannonball fragments and various pieces of buckles and tackle for uniforms and horse harnesses. While these objects may not have been haunted by an actual spirit, I believed that they could be used to connect with the spirit world. The history of the land and the Civil War battle was well-documented by erected historical markers just outside of the house, courtesy of the State of Tennessee. However, the paranormal investigation team was able to uncover an earlier antebellum history about the property that was even more intriguing.

A few miles down Franklin Pike from where our house sat, there was a shopping strip containing a grocery store and restaurants. Before the Civil War, all the land between the strip and our house belonged to a wealthy planter. The mansion once stood on the hill where the shopping plaza is now located. It was torn down to build the current shopping strip.

This farm had approximately one hundred registered slaves who worked in the fields. According to an old map from the Tennessee Historical Archives, the location of the slave cabins would have been where our house now stands, next to the creek. There is no surviving record of the specific crops grown on this land during the antebellum period, but the primary crop in Tennessee during that time was cotton. Another profitable business for large property owners in the area during this period was raising horses. Ironically, I had a bucket full of old horse tackle rings that I picked up from metal detecting. It was very likely that the property may have had horses as well. After the Civil War, tobacco became one of the most common crops grown on Nashville-area farms, continuing into the present day.

Cotton was indeed a highly profitable crop in high demand, both nationally and internationally, before the Civil War. Many plantation owners in the region invested heavily in its cultivation. Slaves were often forced to work long hours in the fields, picking cotton by hand and using machines to process the raw cotton into bales for transport. Written accounts describe how pickers' fingers bled into the cotton due to cuts caused by picking the seeds out of the spiky bolls of cotton before the cotton could be processed by machines.

With so much history spanning nearly a century of slavery and the scars of a Civil War battle, it wasn't difficult to understand why the paranormal investigators believed the land could release negative energy to anyone who ventured onto it. Their proposed solution was to have the house cleansed by a priest and for me to cease any engagement with the spirit world immediately.

One thing that bothered me during this consultation was Janet's outright accusatory tone, blaming me for all the activity in the house. Her attitude was that I should have known better, and she concluded that I had opened the doorway to the activity in the house. Naturally, this attitude didn't sit well with me. It also bothered me that they suggested a catholic priest, just because my father was from a catholic family. She believed that our ancestors would intervene in a spiritual battle on our behalf. But I was not a Catholic at the time, nor was I practicing Judaism, as my mother's side of the family was Jewish. Being more of a spiritualist at heart, I studied more Wiccan crafts and felt a priest was a little inappropriate, but I went along with the suggestion for the sake of my roommate. She was not a catholic either, but she felt that having a blessing done by a priest was a good course of action.

After the paranormal investigation, several things began to change with the activity in the house. It felt like the calm before a storm, just waiting to unleash its full force. As the days passed, I became increasingly introverted and filled with anger. I started using digital recorders, not to capture evidence anymore, but to attempt direct communication with the spirits. It never failed to captivate me. Disregarding all of Janet's suggestions and accusations, I dove headfirst into exploring the depths of the darkness. My daily activities became a dance with the spiritual realm, leading me down a path of profound darkness. I set up makeshift altars in my room adorned with both voodoo and Wiccan sigils, trying to appease the spirits and draw them out further, much like I had witnessed a man do in New Orleans.

Late one evening, a new friend I had made at Tish's shop and coffee bar came to my house to personally experience the paranormal activity that had consumed my life. He himself dabbled in the occult and ritualistic magic and had an insatiable curiosity for the unexplained. He thought it would be an exciting adventure to try a séance in my back closet, the epic center for activity and the neighboring apartment, which remained empty up to that point.

I had never ventured into the realm of séances before, and the idea of conducting one seemed both exhilarating and eerie. It promised a unique way to spend a Friday night, a night filled with the unknown and the possibility of contacting the other side. As my friend and I gathered in the dimly lit closet, our hearts raced with anticipation, unaware of the profound consequences our decision would unleash upon our lives. I had an antique Ouija board from the mid-'70s, a relic of a bygone era that I carefully set up between us, its weathered wooden surface and eerie lettering adding an extra layer of mystique to the atmosphere.

The board had a strange static tingly sensation on my fingertips as we both positioned ourselves around it, crossed legged on the floor, our fingers lightly resting on the planchette, ready to contact the entity lingering in the shadows. The room remained shrouded in silence, with only the soft, rhythmic ticking of an old wall clock counting down the moments until the unknown would unveil its secrets to us.

The room held the familiar haziness that had become part of our encounters with paranormal activity in the house. To deepen the atmosphere, I darkened the room by turning off the lights, unplugging the night lights I had grown accustomed to, and lit just one solitary candle. The energy in the house that night was already oppressive, but an eerie and chilling sensation ran down my spine as our fingertips gently touched the planchette. It felt as though an electric current was coursing through me.

As I completed these preparations, I entered a trance-like state, a meditative dissociation that allowed me to experience what I referred to as "flashes." These flashes were rapid glimpses of past events in each space or fleeting encounters with entities from the spirit realm. During this trance, I saw mere seconds of a man trudging through the woods, carrying what seemed to be a musket slung over his shoulder. In his hands, he held several pelts from various animals.

Simultaneously, the planchette moved silently across the Ouija board, spelling out words that appeared to be in French. However, to both of us, it came across as gibberish. We pondered whether this was the communication of a French trapper from a bygone era or something more sinister, such as a demonic entity masquerading as French speech. The enigma remained unsolved, but my friend grew increasingly uncomfortable and insisted on ending the session after only a few exchanged words.

As the days passed, the energy within the house seemed to intensify, taking on a darker and more malevolent presence. My mood also darkened in tandem with this escalating negativity. Shadows that darted across door frames and through hallways became a daily occurrence, their movements entirely independent of any discernible light source. Often billowy in form, these shadows were large enough to block out the light itself.

Objects continued their inexplicable movements, with keys and money mysteriously moving to places where they had not been left. The very air in the house felt oppressively heavy, as if an unseen force was bearing down upon it. I found myself becoming increasingly withdrawn, consumed by anger, and plagued by bouts of deep depression. To make matters worse, this malevolent energy seemed to cling to anyone who set foot in the house, leaving them unsettled and affected by its eerie presence.

The paranormal investigators had convinced my roommate that we needed to have the house blessed by an ordained Catholic priest. As mentioned earlier, I was not in favor of this course of action but went with it for my roommate's sake. She had a friend at the time who had just been ordained in the Catholic Church and who came to the house. He was not a demonologist, nor was he interested in becoming one, but he was more focused on listening to the house's problems and blessing the house in spiritual service. Upon his arrival, he was met immediately by a dark force which he said made him physically ill. Whatever entity was there, it did not want him in the house.

He sat down for a moment as my roommate explained the haunting occurrences. I remained silent, though his presence stirred a deep anger within me. Sensing my mood, he rose to begin his service, leaving me to my thoughts. Slowly, he made his way around the house's perimeter, methodically moving from room to room. In one hand, he clutched a small silver container filled with holy water, and in the other, he held a wooden cross. His head was bowed in prayer, and his lips moved silently as he murmured incantations.

As he walked, he flicked droplets of holy water onto the

walls and floors, making the sign of the cross with his free hand to bless the house and all those who dwelled within it. The water glistened in the dim light, casting tiny droplets of light across the room. With each step, the priest's pace quickened, his movements becoming more fluid and confident. He appeared to grow taller and stronger, as if an otherworldly power surged through him and infused the very essence of the house. When he reached the threshold of my room at the back of the house, he paused for a moment before entering, as if sensing something unusual or unsettling within its confines.

After the house blessing, the priest would later recount how the air around him had grown heavy and thick, as though a great weight had descended upon the room. His voice rose in volume, echoing off the walls, as he spoke with firm, unwavering authority, commanding whatever presence he felt in the back of the house to depart.

Ultimately, he reached the final corner of the house, my walk-in closet, standing before the door where the shadow had been captured by the paranormal investigators. With a final, decisive gesture, he sprinkled holy water over the threshold and whispered a concluding prayer, sealing the space with protection against the malevolent forces that had plagued it for so long. I never told him that I had found a set of rosary beads tucked beneath a shelf along the wall that separated the empty apartment from ours. In truth, I had forgotten about this discovery all together until the priest talked about his experience in that room.

The air seemed to lighten, and calm descended over the house. The anger drained from my body. I immediately felt better! I was so thankful for him.

He left me a plastic set of rosary beads by my bedside after I told him I saw shadows running along my bedroom walls toward the closet. Before he left, he turned and faced my room, his eyes scanning the walls and floors as if searching for any lingering signs of evil or malevolence. But there was nothing there - only the faint scent of incense he had previously burned and his steady breathing during his visit. He left feeling confident, and we did too.

The house seemed to shimmer and glow with a newfound radiance, as if blessed with a divine light that would protect it for years. Sadly, this temporary relief would only last a short while. In fact, the energy seemed to intensify and become more malevolent after the priest's visit, as if his presence incited the entity.

– Chapter 7 –

LORE vs. ENERGY

"I believe, after reading a real account of the Spirit's visit to the Bells' home, one must know it was not just "superstition of the times." A person of reason likely would doubt that such performances could have been carried on by a human being. Could it be so performed at the present time, when we are so far advanced in sleight-of-hand, telepathy, and electricity?" — Charles Bailey Bell (A Descendant)."

As the cold settled outside, subtle noises within the house became a constant presence, and the objects that moved did so with escalating violence. It was as if some malevolent force had seized control of the house and was now venting its wrath on anyone who dared to enter. Visitors to the house often felt drained and deeply disturbed, as if a piece of them had been taken when they left. Even those who were skeptical of ghosts and hauntings could sense the overwhelming negative energy permeating the house, leading many to avoid it entirely. Friends ceased to visit, and I grew increasingly isolated. The few people I considered my family became my only connection to the outside world.

Instead of going out with friends to dinners and parties, I found myself spending my evenings alone at home, immersed in darkened rooms softly illuminated by the gentle flicker of candles. These moments allowed me to feel the energy of the spirit world flowing around me. My fascination with the mysteries of the unknown and the potential existence of a realm beyond our physical world had always held me in its grip. However, this newfound obsession with the spirit world consumed me entirely, leading me down a path of exploration and discovery that would come to define my entire existence.

During this period, I was consumed by a desire to explore the paranormal, launching on a binge of haunted locations across Tennessee. I eagerly sought out any place that would allow me to step through its doors and delve into the mysteries of the spirit world. My new friend from Tish's shop, who was aware of my passion for collecting paranormal experiences and my deep interest in the occult joined me in some of these spirit expeditions.

This new friend had a unique proposition for me: the chance to spend a night investigating the infamous Bell Witch Cave in Adams, Tennessee. Even though the expensive cave tours offered to tourists seemed somewhat trivial compared to the other haunted locations I had visited by then, the captivating folklore surrounding the cave was too enticing to resist. However, one major hurdle to accepting the cave as a genuinely haunted location was the fact that the actual Bell Witch Cave was located miles away from where the Bell's Cabin had stood.

Adams, Tennessee is a small, picturesque town nestled in the rolling hills of the Cumberland Plateau. The town is known for its lush, green countryside, dotted with charming farms and rustic barns, as well as its haunted history dating back to the early 1800s. While driving through the area, the air was filled with smoke that smelled of dried tobacco leaves during the curing process. Many of the barns had drying tobacco leaves hanging inside them, with a flu lit to keep the barn at a stable temperature to cure the leaves. Billows of smoke from this process dotted the landscape on all the nearby farms, giving the crisp Autumn afternoon an unforgettable smell.

The locals are not overly welcoming either. Just before you arrive at the turnoff for the Bell Witch Cave property sits a churchyard with a cemetery attached to it containing slave burials. We pulled off to look at the cemetery and try to piece together some of the history and lore surrounding the Bell Witch Farm. Within fifteen minutes of walking through the gravestones, an elderly man dressed in tattered overalls pulls up in a beat-up pickup truck resembling a character out of a Stephen King novel. He hurriedly got out of his truck and began to yell at us that this was private property, demanding to know who we were. After telling him we were spending the night at the cave, he tried to tell us that we did not have permission to do this either and had to leave the area immediately. He must have been some local police dog without holding the proper credentials. We left after the encounter but can assure the readers that the church grounds are not labeled as private property and are open to the public. We ignored him and went on about our business at hand.

The property on which the Bells Witch Cave tours are run did not appear to have any part in the local agriculture. Instead, they appeared to make their money from selling tours of the Cave and hosting haunted hayrides and bonfires. A cabin on the property was a replica of what the Bell's family cabin was like. This cabin was the focal point and check-in for all tours.

Once inside, one of the owners of the property welcomed us and told us about the history and folklore surrounding the property. As she talked, I looked over a notebook full of photographs of orbs and light streaks taken over the years by guests visiting the property. Most of the photographs could have easily been explained because of camera straps, wayward fingers from the photographer and light refractions.

One of the more prominent stories is Andrew Jackson visiting the Bells to witness the activity. However, upon further research, this story appears to be just legend. John Bell, who was involved in local politics, was running for State office at the time of Andrew Jackson's visit. This information is directly available in the old journals of Andrew Jackson located at the Tennessee State Archives in downtown Nashville. Andrew Jackson endorsed John Bell for office and frequently visited the Bells to plan elections and political strategies.

With this information, I was disappointed in the Bell Witch Story after my first visit and research. If anything, it's a good example of how some paranormal investigators can misinterpret a location and run their "evidence" based on false information. However, during my visit, I did flip to one photo in the binder of spooky images that caught my attention immediately. Out of hundreds of prints, just one jumped out. The image was a black shadow about three feet tall, standing in an empty field on the property. Of course, as is the case with so much presented evidence in the paranormal world, the image was pixelated and blurry. The shadow appeared to be a large animal, almost like a large black dog. A ghostly black dog is one of the top reported paranormal occurrences in Adams, Tennessee today, and was very much reported during the Bell's infamous haunting by the Bells. This photograph can be seen in the collection of images taken on the Bell Witch Property in their museum and shop.

As I stared at this image in disbelief, the tour guide shifted back to the present, continuing with the tale of the enigmatic Native American skull that had been reportedly found in the Bell Witch Cave by one of the Bell children, who then brought it back to the cabin. This infamous skull was said to have initiated the haunting. What piqued my interest about this narrative, however, was that when I perused the actual journals of John Adams, people mentioned visiting Bell's farm to witness the paranormal activity, but there was no mention of the cave. Moreover, the enigmatic skull's absence from the journals left me contemplating whether this tale had indeed been concocted and subsequently woven into the legend over time. It's worth noting that the first documented occurrence of this story appears to be in the writings of a descendant of John Bell, Charles Bailey Bell, in his work *The Bell Witch of Tennessee*, penned during the 1930s.

It's crucial to acknowledge that the notion of Native American burial grounds being associated with hauntings is a recurring theme in paranormal research. So often in hauntings, investigators are quick to blame a haunting on Native Americans. Here's my theory regarding the origin of this idea:

During the early seventeenth century, Native American tribes inhabiting the East Coast engaged in conflicts with colonial villages and settlements. These clashes were driven by the tribes' efforts to repel white settlers and reclaim their ancestral lands. Many journals and pieces of colonial literature from that period recount stories of "demons" (referring to the Native Americans) raiding small settlements and isolated farms.

The fear that white settlers harbored towards these Indigenous people transformed them into spectral beings and nightmarish apparitions lurking in the dark woods. This fear even extended into their homes, manifesting themselves as night terrors that haunted their dreams. This historical context likely contributed to the association between Native American burial grounds and hauntings in later folklore and paranormal narratives.

One such chilling story from the 1600s revolves around a young girl named Abigail Williams. In the year 1662, Abigail, who happened to be the niece of the notorious Reverend Samuel Parris, resided in Salem Village alongside her relatives. Her parents, Joseph and Abigail Rogers, had tragically met their demise in an Indian raid that had targeted the small settlement they hailed from in Maine. It's worth noting that historical records at the Peabody Institute Library suggest that Abigail was not an only child; she may have also witnessed the tragic loss of her siblings during the same harrowing raid.

During this period in Puritan Society, Native Americans had already become a source of intense fear and folklore. In the annals of old literature and historical records, Native Americans were often referred to as devils and demons who roamed the dense forests by night. Despite being the Indigenous people defending their rightful lands, they were regarded as a formidable and terrifying force along the East Coast seaboard.

These historical events laid the foundation for the enduring folklore of haunted Native American burial grounds, a narrative that would be retold and passed down through generations across America for centuries to come. It's become almost a paranormal staple for investigators to attribute land hauntings as a direct result of Native Americans.

There are several accounts of the Bell property being land taken directly from the Chickasaws. Reportedly, this tribe conducted raids up and down the Red River to reclaim their ancestral lands when anyone residing outside the populated villages and cities was isolated. With no long-distance communication, most cities and villages operated as isolated silos, and the primary means of communication was traveling by foot. It's easy to speculate that the sole source of entertainment would have been gathering by the fireplace at night to share tales or engage in reading.

Given that the Salem Witch trials occurred nearly two centuries before the events on the Bell's property at the beginning of the 19th Century, it's not unreasonable to consider that tales of Native American hauntings were circulating, especially among those living alongside the Chickasaw tribe. In every settlement along the East Coast, isolated from major city hubs, a similar theme may have prevailed. The notion that Native American burial grounds could potentially impart a lethal curse upon any white individual who inadvertently ventured onto their sacred grounds is likely a product of colonialism. I am not suggesting that these hauntings do not occur, but that we may need to look more closely as investigators at the facts against such claims.

Returning to the present and the Bell Witch Cave, I spent the night there and didn't encounter anything negative that I could attribute to a witch. Instead, what I personally experienced was a static energy permeating the cave, akin to a low vibrational frequency that could be sensed if one focused on it. The accounts from those who tour this cave often include reports of growling, scratching, whispering, and even peculiar animal sounds. However, in my case, the cave's phenomena paled in comparison to what was unfolding in my own home. One other detail about my experience in the Bell Witch Cave is that the gravesite from where this mysterious Native American head was found was a hole neatly cut out of the surrounding rock, something hardly done by actual Native Americans two centuries ago.

I picked up a rock from the rear of the cave and brought it home to experiment with the claim that taking a rock from the cave would result in the Bell Witch's haunting following you. I placed this rock on an antique dresser in my bedroom and eventually forgot about it. Later in the year, the rock simply vanished. I'm unsure whether one of my friends might have taken it or if it genuinely was haunted and disappeared as an apport back to the cave. (Just a note: "Apport" is a term used in paranormal phenomena for objects disappearing from one place and materializing in another. It's an interesting and eerie phenomenon often associated with hauntings and other unexplained occurrences.)

Reports suggest that coins and even grapes would spontaneously appear for the Bells seemingly out of thin air. While it might be tempting to dismiss such accounts, what makes them intriguing is that some of the coins would originate from foreign countries, and finding grapes in such a remote area would have been challenging. What I found particularly fascinating about the Bell Witch Cave is that the hauntings that occur in the present seem to be nothing more than manifestations of the ghosts that people inadvertently bring with them during their investigations. It was an important lesson for me at this stage, in those conclusions about the haunting in my own home against preconceived prejudices, legends and our own ability to draw energy became a reality.

Another result of visiting this cave is that I explored the idea of psychometry and my own abilities. I began collecting objects from various haunted locations across the country just to see what energy I could pick up from these objects, and if it was possible to create connections through these objects from afar. My collection included a piece of the floor from St. Augustine's lighthouse, where a tragic accident had claimed the lives of three children during the lighthouse's construction. I had acquired bullets found on multiple battleground sites and a voodoo doll from an authentic practitioner in New Orleans, constructed with iron spikes as a safeguard against future hurricanes.

One of my favorite pieces in this collection appeared to be a small fragment of wallpaper from the third floor of the Blue Moon River Brewery in Savannah, Georgia, which was undergoing construction during my visit. A staff member who accompanied me to the third floor at that time recounted a story of a construction worker being pushed down the stairs and severely injured by unseen hands.

It's important to note that these items were not inherently haunted, but they originated from locations imbued with a certain energy. When collected, they had the potential to create an environment conducive to hauntings.

At the time, I didn't realize that I was unwittingly inviting a multitude of different entities and energies into my own life and home. Inadvertently, I was welcoming the unknown with open arms, almost daring any entity to unleash its worst as proof that the paranormal events that had occurred throughout my life held some validation.

The rock from the Bell Witch Cave was kept on my

dresser, a prized object that I valued probably more than what is considered healthy by modern health consultants. Up until it suddenly disappeared that is. While it was in my possession, I didn't think much about the consequences of having it at the time. The rock itself had a reddish hue and felt heavy in the palm of my hand, consisting mainly of raw iron. When held, it gave off a strange slight vibrational energy. It became a showpiece when people visited. For me, the cave procured very little evidential activity and was more of a "created haunting" for tourism.

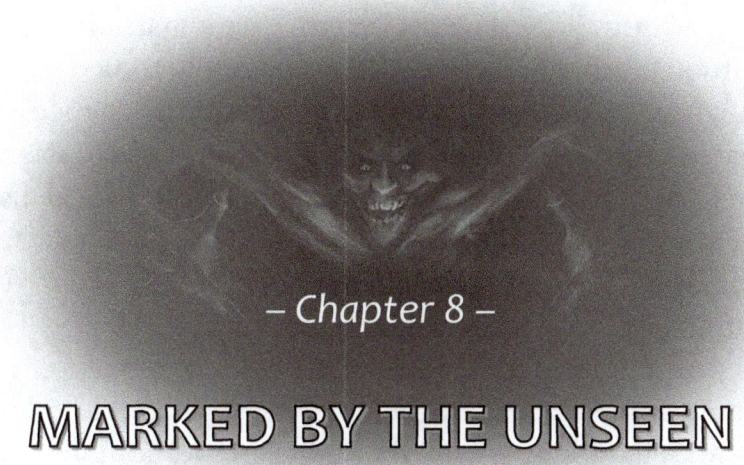

– Chapter 8 –

MARKED BY THE UNSEEN

"Haunted by the past, touched by the unseen, and marked by the spirit." — Unknown

Several investigations I took part in left me feeling emotionally numb and withdrawn. I found myself becoming increasingly irritable, a stark reminder of my past relationship. Petty arguments would escalate, leading to outbursts at my roommate for no apparent reason. A series of unfortunate events seemed to follow me, and I began to feel physically unwell.

As someone who had been an avid runner and a health-conscious gym enthusiast, I was taken aback by my sudden struggles with daily routines. I found myself utterly exhausted and breathless during even a simple one-mile hike. Running my usual mileage became impossible, and I started experiencing strange body aches, constant headaches, night sweats, and limb fatigue. At the time, I attributed these symptoms to the natural process of aging (I was approaching twenty-nine) and disrupted sleep caused by the paranormal activity in my life. Events in my personal life took a tumultuous turn. I underwent job changes, grappled with the stress of writing dissertations and career path changes, and navigated through other challenging life circumstances. Amidst the chaos, I sought solace in visiting local parks, frequenting Tish's shop, and dedicating myself to curating a photography gallery showcasing my work from New Orleans.

At home, I perpetually sensed a presence enveloping me. I became apprehensive of the darkness and could no longer bring myself to sleep with the lights off. One night, while alone in the house, I had a night light on as I lay in bed. Despite the crisp, late-fall weather with temperatures in the low fifties outside, the room grew uncomfortably warm— a sensation that had often preceded paranormal events. I could feel the presence close by, and I listened intently to the strange rustling sound that often manifested in my room. With my eyes, I could almost trace the source of the sound as it moved across the room.

I was repeatedly awoken by the sensation of something sitting down on the bed. During the initial occurrences, I assumed it was my twenty-pound Burmese cat, Dmitri. However, each time this phenomenon transpired, the bed would shake slightly, and there would be a noticeable indentation on the far corner—slightly heavier than my cat would be. Startled, I would jump up suddenly, only to discover that Dmitri wasn't even in the room with me. His refusal to sleep in my room was yet another concerning sign that I chose to disregard. Whenever these paranormal events unfolded, the room would become unbearably hot, prompting me to open the sliding glass door to let in some cold air and cool down the room.

These occurrences kept up for the next few weeks until I

got so tired that I started sleeping during all hours of the day, fitting in naps where I could. Feeling exhausted and unwell, depression soon overwhelmed me. Every night became a battle with me wondering why these things were happening. I became broken and blamed myself for not only the current events, but also of all of the past abuse I had undergone growing up. Thoughts of suicide started to echo through my mind repeatedly. I felt defeated in my education, my life's direction and felt as though I was a failure. All the cards were stacked against me in the game of life.

On one such night that I was experiencing an especially strong bout of depression, I was distracted by the sound of rustling in my room, just several feet from where I was sitting on my bed. Following the sound, it sounded as though it had moved into the closet, away from me. Suddenly, anger overtook me. I stood next to the bed and screamed at the entity! My poor cat ran from under my bed and shot out of the room. I jumped in fear as he ran past my feet. Expecting relief, I was suddenly overtaken by a feeling of something standing in the doorway of my closet. I went to run out of the room after my cat, but as I did so, I caught my gym bag out of the corner of my eye just as it slammed into the door where Dmitri just ran out of, the contents spewing out onto the floor. The gym bag sailed by its own accord across the room. Shocked, I got out of my room.

This bag was not light, as it contained swimming gear, shampoo, running shoes, and a bunch of other items I used throughout the week during my workouts at the gym. It was always kept on a hook on the back of the bathroom door. How had it managed to unhook itself, and fly all the way across the room into the door frame to the hallway? It slammed into the side of the door frame with such force that the shampoo bottle spilled open, making a mess all over the wall and carpet. A small metal combination lock was also inside the bag and could have seriously injured my cat had the bag hit him directly. At the time, my cat was one of the few things that I loved, aside from my closest friends.

My relationships were deteriorating, as well as my physical health. I felt isolated and completely alone. The paranormal investigators were of no help to the situation, nor had any answers to how to make the paranormal stop. Instead, they blamed me for the activity and said it was just a matter of tuning it out that would stop it. The priest only seemed to make the activity much more hostile. To this, I have no answer to why this happened, other than, if a negative entity was present, the attack would be more vicious toward a positive leader, as if you took out the leaders.

I began to feel stalked by shadows, both in my dreams and in real life. There seemed to be no way out.

Amid this unnerving series of events, few could match the profound dread that consumed me just before Thanksgiving. It was another chilly night, and I found myself alone in my apartment, the clock nearing 3:00 AM. Much like many previous nights, I was abruptly awakened, but this time, it was different. My bed trembled slightly, as if an earthquake were rattling through. That's exactly what I believed was occurring at that moment. I sat up hastily, alarmed by the sensation. However, to my bewilderment, nothing appeared to be happening. The strange vibration ceased, and the room returned to an eerie silence. I reluctantly lay back down, attempting to dismiss the bizarre occurrence. I pulled the covers tightly over me, shutting my eyes in fear of what I might encounter. Again, the room grew stifling hot, as if the entity was stirring the energy in the room. I began to sweat from the intense heat. Finally, when I couldn't take it anymore, I threw off the blanket and yelled,

"Stop!'

Before I could even utter the whole word, I was suddenly gripped by a searing sensation running down the left side of my thigh. Startled and fearing it might be an insect bite or something worse, I leaped out of bed. My anxiety drove me to hastily strip all the bedding off my bed, shaking everything out in a frantic search for whatever might have caused it. To my confusion, there was absolutely nothing to be found. The burning sensation persisted on my leg, feeling as though it was radiating from beneath the skin in an inexplicable manner. I noticed three small, raised welts running about an inch down the outer side of my thigh, just above the knee cap. These welts were minuscule and resembled the marks that might be made by a small rodent, such as a possum or a raccoon. They hadn't broken the skin, but they remained red and raised for nearly a day afterward.

After that unsettling incident, I delved into research about scratches and welts attributed to paranormal encounters on the internet. I had long held the belief that the paranormal couldn't manifest physical effects on a person. At the time, there wasn't much information available on this subject. I grew increasingly apprehensive about sleeping in the house and started taking longer trips out of town. In some inexplicable way, I felt as though I had been marked.

My initial thought was whether the Bell Witch Cave rock I had kept on my dresser might be connected to these strange occurrences. Often, once an item is in your possession, it tends to fade into the background of your daily routine, and you don't give it much thought. Similarly, this mysterious rock had become a part of the background of my life. However, when I considered its potential connection to the recent strange events, I decided to remove it from my bedroom, just in case it was somehow contributing to the activity.

My plan was to place it outside by the creek. To my astonishment, which is when I discovered the rock had disappeared. My roommate insists she hadn't seen the rock for weeks leading up to its disappearance, and no one ever admitted to taking it. It was as if it had simply vanished into thin air.

– Chapter 9 –

A WITCH'S BATTLE

"Magic comes from what is inside you. It is part of you. You can't weave together a spell that you don't believe in."
— Jim Butcher

During that same week following the incident, I reached out to Tish and shared the latest developments regarding the scratches. She expressed genuine concern for my well-being and promptly arranged a house call with a group of psychic mediums, healers, and paranormal investigators who all participated in mediumship circles at her shop in Nashville.

As they arrived, I noticed they were all dressed in ordinary clothing. For some reason, I had expected them to appear in long robes and hoods, akin to what I had witnessed my neighbor wearing just a few months ago when she attended her Summer's Eve ritual. It was clear that this group of individuals defied conventional societal norms. I welcomed them in, and Tish wasted no time. She headed straight to my bedroom, tossing her bag onto my bed as soon as she entered the room. Without hesitation, she turned her attention to the closet door.

"So, you enjoy frightening young women?" Tish called out, addressing the entity whose presence was undoubtedly lingering somewhere in the room. The room still bore a heavy atmosphere, indicating that something was indeed present, although I couldn't discern its location at that moment. I prepared myself for a potential magical showdown between the witch and an irate spirit, whether it be a human or something else entirely.

There was no audible response emanating from anywhere in the house, not even the typical rustling noises that I had grown accustomed to when I was alone. Nevertheless, Tish seemed to pinpoint the spirit's location with ease, as if an invisible person shared the room with us. Meanwhile, the rest of her entourage settled into seats around the living room and dining room in the front part of the house, patiently awaiting further instruction.

"You better back off from the girls living here," she declared, though her choice of words wasn't particularly polite. Her conversation with the unseen entity continued for nearly fifteen minutes, almost resembling an argument with a spirit. What she conspicuously refrained from doing was issuing threats, provoking, or attempting to further agitate the spirit. Following the exchange, she explained that if a spirit has already lived and passed away, they have presumably learned from their earthly experiences, and humans have no authority to pass further judgment upon them. Such judgments, she asserted, were the purview of the Spirit alone.

Tish continued to describe the spirit as a tall, slender man with a beard who likely lived during the early years of the 20th century. This description bore a striking resemblance to the hat man shadow figure I had encountered months earlier.

It led me to formulate a new theory regarding the hat man phenomenon. Could it be that this commonly reported entity is simply a manifestation of a male spirit from the turn of the century? Shadow figures are a frequent occurrence in paranormal manifestations, often appearing as silhouettes. If this hypothesis holds true, it raises the question of whether the common attire of men during the Victorian and early 20th-century periods, characterized by long dark coats and top hats, might account for the prevalence of the "hat man" in paranormal encounters.

For nearly an hour, Tish immersed herself in the energy of the room. It wasn't just the man's presence; there were multiple spirits coming and going, as if sharing a common space between the living and the dead. Her focus shifted to the closet area, where she proposed the existence of a doorway that led to the other side of the house. This side of the house had remained vacant since my neighbor's passing months earlier. It seemed plausible, given its alignment with the hallway that ran straight through our apartment. Tish speculated that the paranormal activity was flowing in and out through this doorway, as if it were still open.

In the scenario where my neighbor was engaging in ritualistic activities to summon various spirits and magical experiences, it would have been reasonable to assume that this energy might have passed through our shared space. This was especially plausible if someone else in the house was inadvertently drawing in this energy. It appeared that I might have been unintentionally attracting this energy through a combination of my psychic abilities, my insatiable curiosity and involvement with the paranormal, and my emotional turmoil during that time. I was also into collecting haunted objects and practicing psychometry, participating in a questionable voodoo ritual in New Orleans, and becoming deeply engrossed in spirit communication, going far beyond mere curiosity.

On that evening, the group gathered in my living room and conducted a healing circle, focusing on providing spiritual healing for me rather than just clearing the house of negative energy. While there are differing opinions about the efficacy of sage cleansing, with some arguing that it should only be performed by Native Americans, Tish used sage to cleanse my room and my aura that night. Additionally, she conducted a simple ritual aimed at bolstering my spiritual and mental strength.

You have articulated a valuable insight: the power of magical items, like sage, candles, or other tools, often lies not in the objects themselves, but in the intention behind their use. Your experience highlights that true magic emanates from within, drawn out by intention and a connection to the spiritual realm. This lesson you've learned about the significance of intention and spiritual connection is indeed crucial when dealing with the spirit world and seeking peace.

It's interesting to see how your perspective on the entity and the negative energy in the house has evolved over time. Sometimes, with more experience and reflection, we gain a deeper understanding of paranormal occurrences and their possible causes. It's a testament to your growth and continued exploration of the spiritual realm. Your ongoing journey in this realm is filled with intriguing insights and experiences.

It's remarkable how the presence of the group of psychic mediums, healers, and paranormal investigators had such a positive and calming effect on your home. Their energy and efforts seemed to bring a sense of peace and lightness to the house, which was a stark contrast to the previous experiences. It's intriguing how these paranormal occurrences seem to ebb and flow, and your journey through them continues to be filled with unexpected twists and turns.

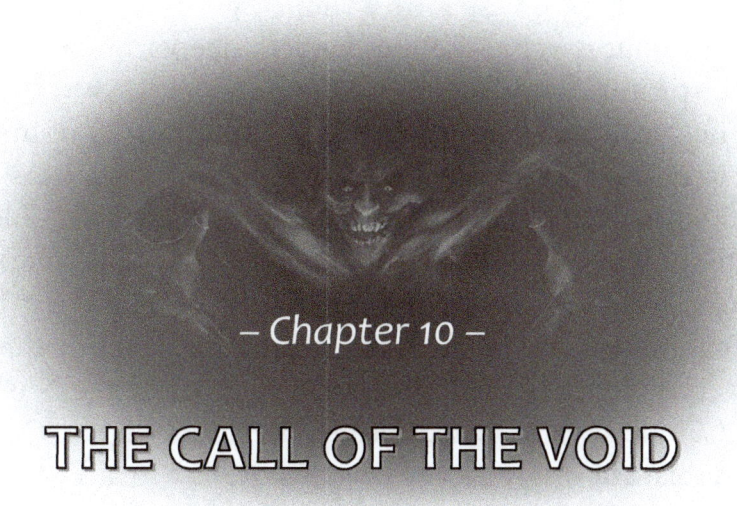

– Chapter 10 –

THE CALL OF THE VOID

"If you look long enough into the void, the void begins to look back through you."
— Friedrich Nietzsche

Exploring your psychic abilities at a known haunted location like the old Nashville City Cemetery sounds like a fascinating experience. The idea of practicing mediumship in such a historically rich and potentially spiritually active place could provide valuable insights into your psychic development and connection with the spirit world. It's a testament to your curiosity and determination in exploring the paranormal realm.

Walking silently around the tombstones in the old Nashville City Cemetery as a part of the mediumship circle's practice sounds like a unique and meditative approach to sensing spiritual energy. It's a way to attune your psychic abilities to the energies of the deceased and the history contained within the cemetery. Exploring such places with a group of like-minded individuals can be a powerful way to enhance your psychic skills and gain a deeper understanding of the spiritual world.

The Nashville City Cemetery is the oldest continuously operated public cemetery in Nashville and contains over 20,000 burials, including revolutionary and civil war soldiers, penitentiary burials, slaves and later free African Americans, mayors, founders of the city of Nashville, and even Fisk's original jubilee singers. It was the perfect place for this sort of exercise in mediumship. Another aspect of the Nashville City Cemetery is its proximity to the ruins of Fort Negley, whose historical significance as a Civil War fortification and a symbol of Union occupation in Nashville is remarkable. It stands as a testament to the impact of war on the region, and a vivid reminder of the Battle of Nashville and the broader Civil War era.

Exploring a cemetery with the intention of practicing spirit communication can be both eerie and enlightening. The sudden drop in temperature and the feeling of chills are often associated with paranormal encounters. It's interesting how certain areas within cemeteries can elicit stronger spiritual connections or sensations. For those seeking to develop their own abilities, this exercise seems like a valuable opportunity in honing their mediumship skills and connecting with the energy of the deceased.

Letting my intuition guide me, I walked down a footpath a few feet before diverting off across the graves, almost feeling pulled toward an old grave, half sunken into the ground beneath a large oak tree. It stood by itself under the shadow of the tree, the engraved writing mostly unintelligible, worn by the last century of weather. Standing on the soft ground before the grave, I took a moment to take in what was coming to me psychically. Then I saw him. A thin middle-aged man, visibly worn by life, stood before me, his pale eyes looking at me from beneath what appeared to be a wool fedora. The imagery only lasted a few seconds, like a flash. And then I heard him.

"My life is easier than yours," he said.

Somehow, I felt as if he had passed from some sort of lung condition, but there is no way to prove that the person buried in this now unmarked grave is indeed the man I saw. However, it was what he said that would stick with me for years. His words resonated with the experiences I was going through, as though this entity was connecting with me on a spiritual and psychic level.

I was still battling a downward spiral of depression, seemingly without any valid cause. Thoughts of suicide flooded through me, like an endless call to the void. Despite having many positive aspects in my life, I struggled to extricate myself from the profound and gloomy feelings of desolation. My thoughts were entirely consumed by the supernatural, becoming the sole subject capable of retaining my focus for more than a mere five minutes.

The activity in my house continued. During the worst nights in which I would stay up all night weeping, I saw another four-foot hooded shadow, much like the shadow the investigators caught on film, run down my hallway. Ironically, that same week, I saw the same figure again, this time in the middle of the road that ran through a wooded section, while I was driving home one night from a friend's house in Bellevue.

These black cloaked figures did not possess a face, nor did they have any form other than a black cloak and only stood around four feet tall. After the second sighting, I associated the hooded dark figure as something more sinister, as the only times it has shown up in my life were during my darkest moments. Its presence was intimidating, foreboding, and downright terrifying. The last time I encountered this figure it was right after a key event in my life that would forever change the course of my life.

Struggling with sleeplessness due to lingering anxieties, I found myself questioning the reasons behind the ongoing turmoil in my life. Adding to my challenges, my health wasn't in the best state. Amidst these struggles, one consistent aspect I maintained was running. During that period, I regularly participated in runs with a community of fellow enthusiasts known as the "East Nasties," a renowned running club based in East Nashville. Our routine involved weekly training sessions, often covering around six miles before reconvening at a local brewery. These gatherings served a dual purpose: they prepared us for upcoming team races and evolved into a valuable social hub throughout my years of residing in Nashville.

It was during these runs that I noticed that I was physically unwell. In just a few short weeks, I found myself winded, unable to finish the runs, and over tired after. My recovery time after each run became greater, and my running time began to be noticeably longer. Everyone I knew suggested that I go see a physician just to be checked out.

During the doctor's visit, I was given a full blood panel test and called back immediately for discussion of the results. Not thinking much of it, I returned to my doctor's office for consultation, not realizing the news they had in store. My blood count markers were extremely high, and I had a lump in my throat.

Everything came to a head at that moment in my life. I was diagnosed with aggressive stage two throat cancer. I couldn't find a reason to continue life. Sleeping in the darkness made me uneasy, and I had a persistent sensation of being pursued by an invisible presence within my own house, wearing away at me gradually.

Within just two weeks, I found myself undergoing surgery and meeting a team of new physicians, including an oncologist, a radiologist, and an endocrinologist. The introduction of the "C" word into my life marked an entire new era, as life would never be the same. I went very quickly through the five stages of grief, in the case of loss of health. Anger followed denial; despair followed anger; and acceptance followed despair; only to end back at the beginning of the cycle. I couldn't understand why all of this was happening to me. I wanted it all to end. I felt like I was on a runaway train heading toward disaster, helpless to get off.

While I was in the hospital recovering from surgery, my roommate took the initiative to assemble a group of our friends for a meeting with our landlord. Thankfully, he understood our situation and graciously allowed us to terminate the lease, enabling us to transition to a different rental property. The new place, located not far from our previous one, had recently undergone renovations and was impeccably clean. This environment was ideal for my recovery during radiation treatments, minimizing the risk of exposure to molds and bacteria. By the time I was discharged from the hospital, I returned to a fresh apartment, a different room, and the unsettling experiences finally came to an end. Before I moved in, Tish had blessed the property, as well as our clergy friend, just for good measure.

– Chapter 11 –

GHOST SICKNESS

"Illnesses caused by ghosts may be physical or mental, though unexplainable by modern Western medicine, as mentioned earlier. Therefore, to treat these illnesses, other measures have to be taken, for instance, praying to a particular god, seeking the aid of a local healer, or appeasing the spirit." — Wu Mingren

Many people disclaim that negative attachments, hauntings, and other spirit phenomena can cause a physical illness, yet, accounts of these experiences are so common, that they have been featured on various paranormal streaming shows over the past few years.

One of the more popular shows on the mainstreaming networks featured an interview with a woman who believed that her time spent in a haunted location as an employee had such a profound impact on her that she developed cancer, a narrative that resonated with my own experiences. Her story hit close to home when she shared her isolation from family and contemplation of suicide—echoing my own struggles living in the haunted house in Nashville.

The oppression she describes started with a mundane job in a haunted hotel, which escalated over the period that she worked in the building. She described the situation as a negative attachment that infiltrated her life and manifested itself into her own life, manifesting its energy through her personal relationship issues and depression. As she told her story, she described her inability to leave the effects of the haunting at her job when she went home after her shift. The Spirit ended up engulfing her life to a degree, infiltrating every aspect of her life. She complained about dealing with depression, which led to more problems in her relationships. Ultimately, she ended up with a cancer diagnosis which she believed to be caused by the energy of the spirit.

It was during a paranormal event at the location in which everything ended for this woman, and she decided to stand up for herself and take back her power. She talks about sitting on the floor with other people, listening to a paranormal investigator speak when an overwhelming wave of suicidal ideation came over her. For her, it was like the spirit was whispering in her ear that she should just get her life over with. Instead of following suit, she stands up, walks out of the hotel and never goes back to work again.

During the summer of 2022, I delved into a case in a remote California hamlet. The call came from a friend in Southern California who invited me along to investigate a private residence out in the countryside east of Sacramento over a weekend to help his team figure out what was going on with the troubling claims of a very distraught homeowner.

Nestled amidst an almond orchard, the unassuming house defied its eerie reputation. The surrounding properties looked like something out of a *Grapes of Wrath* scene by John

Steinbeck, in those fields of lush grapes and orchards surrounded dilapidated wooden farmhouses for miles and miles down narrow country roads. On one stretch of particularly lonely highway, engulfed by fruit trees on both sides, I witnessed a solitary figure climb out of the fields and stumble out into the road in a bright orange tattered shirt and torn jeans, as if he embodied the spirit of survival amidst the echoes of a bygone era.

But this property was different. The two-story farmhouse, built to resemble a Victorian, was well kept and tidy. Outwardly, it boasted lush gardens, an antique water feature and charming artisan decor, exuding an eclectic and welcoming aura. The property's owner, a second-generation landholder, had grown up on the land, though the house itself was a creation of the late 70s. Shortly after her family moved into the new house, supernatural phenomena began to unfold.

Anticipating the team's request for an interview with the client, I arrived ahead of the investigation to prepare. I positioned a camera and a few lights for the homeowner interview. While engrossed in conversation, I caught sight of a fleeting shadow crossing the kitchen window. Uncertainty lingered whether it originated from within or outside the house, momentarily obstructing the light as I was occupied securing an electrical cord with gaffer tape.

During the interview, the owner recalled paranormal events that resemble poltergeist activity, such as disembodied voices, objects being moved around, electronics turning off and on, etc., but there was something she said that reminded me of my own experiences. As she was telling me various stories about the activity, she began to become emotional. She said there was a figure attached to her from a very young age, and would appear in the windows of her house, particularly the window where I had just witnessed the light being blocked just a half hour before the interview.

She led me outside and showed me a place where she saw wet footsteps in the grass after the entity manifested in the window one night during the family's dinner. The house itself was completely private, hemmed in on all sides, including the driveway in, with several acres of mature almond trees. As I listened to her story, I realized that she too, like myself, has felt haunted throughout her life. Her story went on to attribute the loss of two previous husbands and three children to the malevolent activity on her property through various accidents and illnesses. Her surviving children refused to stay in the home. Even as recently as last year, her third husband was battling an illness in hospice.

My overnight investigation revealed a plethora of inexplicable paranormal occurrences within the house. From fleeting two-foot shadows in the orchard to disembodied voices and an unsettling sensation of being watched, the evidence was compelling. The crux lies in her unshakeable belief that these otherworldly phenomena have inflicted both herself and her family with physical ailments, potentially claiming lives in the process.

This leads to a fundamental question: Can the spirit realm not only induce mental distress like depression and anxiety, but also trigger physical maladies, including cancer? An affirmative answer challenges the conventional notion that spirits cannot harm us, particularly those living in physical bodies.

According to certain Native American traditions, the spirit of the deceased can attach itself to a living host, akin to a parasitic relationship. This attachment purportedly saps the host's vitality over time, manifesting as symptoms ranging from appetite loss and weakness to anxiety, depression, and even physical illnesses. In some belief systems, this "ghost sickness" can culminate in death, as the afflicted soul is carried into the realm of the departed by the attaching spirit.

But why would the spirit world want to harm humanity in the first place? The dichotomy between good and evil is a common theme across many faiths, influencing moral and ethical frameworks. Even traditions like Taoism and Buddhism, which emphasize balance and interconnectedness over strict duality, acknowledge negative energy's potential to disrupt one's life when harmony is disrupted.

The interplay of good and evil is a recurring motif across religions. A dynamic between a demonic realm and an angelic one shapes human existence, particularly in the realm of thoughts and actions. This dynamic becomes especially pronounced when considering paranormal phenomena during hauntings and attachments. Strikingly, many affected individuals either have heightened sensitivity to the spirit world or hold roles as "lightworkers," influencing others positively through mentoring, healing, or other abilities. It's as if negative forces are drawn to target the light. In all belief systems, these malevolent forces sap individuals of vital energy, disrupting their spiritual equilibrium. Energy, the life force that courses through all living beings, becomes a target.

But getting back to the initial question of whether an entity, or unseen force, can cause a physical illness: If negative energy can drain this life force and induce periods of stress, fear, and depression, it stands to reason that it could precipitate physical illness. Over extended haunting periods, the intricate interplay between stress and depression could potentially pave the way for a state of "dis-ease" within both body and mind.

The meaning of the word illness according to Mirriam-Webster is simply an unhealthy state of mind and body. The definition includes mind. What's more, the first synonym mentioned under this definition is the word wickedness. First coined in the 1200s in old English and stemming from Old Norse, illness was used to describe something that was morally evil; offensive, objectionable to a person's well-being. In the 1400s, the term was used to describe someone "marked by evil intentions; harmful, pernicious." This did not mean that the person themselves was evil, but that they were a victim of something, or someone else inflicting harm.

When cross referenced through several cultures that had no real connection with one another, at least not during the ones described above, it's curious to note the similarities when considering "ghost sickness". Almost all cultures believe that an unseen force can cause maladies, whether from a physical or mental capacity. To cure these illnesses, the Native American culture practices ceremonial "ghost dances," to release the oppressing spirit, while the catholic church, Judaism and Muslim religions all pray to the saints, angels and to God to achieve the same release.

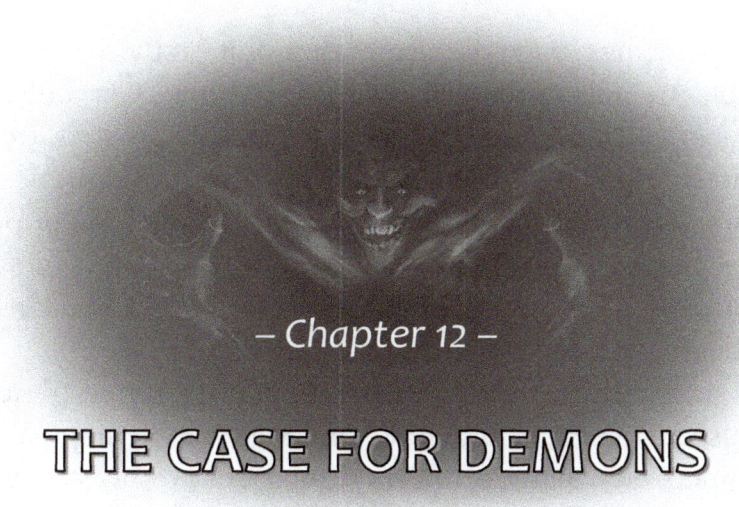

– Chapter 12 –

THE CASE FOR DEMONS

"An insidious, sneaking enemy, who enters the very heart of you, and pretends to be you, with the lie that it is you, – you are accusing yourself–this influence cannot be thrown out or cast down by your own strength." — Arthur Crane

One of the bigger questions raised in this case of the Nashville haunting is whether the oppression was caused by a demonic force. Personally, I felt as if I was, and continue to be, oppressed by the unseen world, but I am unsure whether this case could be considered demonic. However, it could be plausible, as there were a lot of personal experiences and activity that went on that is left unsaid in this book.

Most information that most people have gathered on the demonic in our current age comes from Hollywood. When we think of demon possession, immediately images of head spinning, green projectile vomit, and growling voices speaking ancient Latin flood our minds.

In recent years, the paranormal trend in both television

and online has been to claim demonic activity wherever possible to gain attention and TV ratings. Certainly, the claims of "demon houses" have become a great source of income for many people, creating a wave of demonic case files for television, with paranormal demonologists popping up on nearly every paranormal investigative team in social media, and numerous hair-raising stories centered around hell, death, and lore.

To counter the current paranormal pop culture trends of the past few years, which have included an overexposure of demonic cases, paranormal investigators are now claiming that these cases are so rare. In fact, most, especially self-proclaimed exorcists, say they have never encountered a true demonic entity. So, which is it? Are paranormal investigators backtracking on negative entity cases to stay in tune with current trends? Are these cases truly rare? Or ... is it that we are looking for these negative cases as Hollywood portrayed them?

Season one of *The Holzer Files*, featuring Dave Schrader, Cindy Kaza, and Shane Pittman, includes an episode titled "The Devil in Texas." This episode reopens a case investigated by Hans Holzer in Tyler, Texas, in the 1960s. In this episode, they briefly recap the events of this case and explore what happened to the family, particularly the son, Andy Beaird, over time. Dubbed as Hans's most unfortunate case, the original story was published by Hans Holzer himself in his work *The Phantoms of Dixie*. An entire chapter is dedicated to the case, featuring a first-hand account from Howard Beaird, the father of the household. The rest of the family included his wife, referred to as John, an older sister named Amy who did not live in the house during the reported hauntings, and their twelve-year-old son, Andy.

The case, reportedly Hans's most tragic according to *The*

Holzer Files, begins much like any other, with an otherwise ordinary family moving into a new, ordinary house. This ranch-style house in the small town of Tyler, Texas, was built just a few years before the Beaird family moved in, with only two other tenants occupying the home before them. Before that, the land was part of a Cherokee reservation and was used as a cow pasture.

First, only small events took place, but they were just noticeable enough to draw attention to the energy. The slightest sounds of phantom footsteps in the hallway were heard, knocking on the walls, and the strange occurrence of dead bugs appearing in the bedroom. Next came the odd behavior of John, who underwent a psychiatric breakdown, locking herself in the main bedroom for days at a time. She would light cigarettes and just leave them lying around the house, burning holes into the duvet and mattress.

Just like most poltergeist phenomena, the activity increased with time. John was moved out of the house and into a psychiatric facility. Howard and Andy, who remained in the house, continued to experience paranormal activity, such as a multitude of dead bugs appearing after the lights were turned out, objects moving around the house, and most mysteriously, letters that seemed to apport from the air in a childlike handwriting with encrypted messages.

Disembodied voices from a dozen different spirits began to communicate with Andy Beaird daily. These voices were not heard by Howard, but Howard was able to see the effects of what the voices were saying to Andy. For instance, in Hans's book, Howard recounts that one of the spirits asked to use the telephone. So, his son asked his father's permission for this spirit to use the phone. When Howard said yes, he watched the phone jump off the receiver in midair, as if someone had picked up the phone.

Letters would appear daily from these spirits. One such instance threatened the well-being of Andy through physical force. The spirit called itself Henry Anglin and claimed to have caused many deaths, such as auto accidents, mixing up people's medication, and inducing mental illness. In one of the last letters from this spirit, it states that he is leaving but won't ask Junior (meaning Andy) to go with him and that he (Andy) might kill himself. In that same letter, the spirit continues and says that John is going to become violent.

After a few years of these occurrences, Andy seems to bear the brunt of the activity. His sister Amy, in a later interview with Hans Holzer, says that her brother used to be a happy boy before moving into the home and that he is increasingly troubled, depressed, and isolated. He drops out of school by this time and seems to spend most of his time engaging with these spirits that communicate with him daily.

By the time Hans Holzer gets on this case, the family dog goes through an illness that Howard believes was caused by the spirit world, and ultimately, it dies. A pistol appears in his own drawer, supposedly brought in by one of the spirits. Was this a coincidence meant to drive the people to madness and suicide?

Hans spends time in the house and tries to capture some activity with the new property owners, who aren't very receptive to his work. He is forced to move on from the case as Andy does not connect well with Hans, according to the last interview between Hans and Andy, and the case ends.

But unfortunately, Andy never fully recovers. Years later, the sole surviving family member, Amy, writes a letter that is revealed by the team on *The Holzer Files* during this episode of the horrors her brother went through years later from this haunting, and that it drove him to end his own life for peace.

Though some aspects of this case seem extreme, such as

the letters appearing out of midair, the mention of this case is important because of the way the energy builds on itself. It doesn't start out with nails being coughed up or bed levitating from the floor. For years the phenomena have been just simple noises and occasional occurrences, such as a cabinet door falling off its hinges for no reason, phantom footsteps in the hallways, and knocking on the walls that could be mistaken as the house settling. As time goes by, the wife becomes mentally incapacitated and Andy begins to communicate daily with these spirits, completely in an oppressed situation.

These negative entities manifested themselves slowly over time, attaching to the family mentally. When investigators today make these claims that they have never experienced a case where a negative entity was present, it's fair to ask the question of whether they are doing due diligence in researching the history of the location, the claims in the case, and afterwards in follow ups with the people involved. Perhaps these negative entities do not present themselves in the way investigators expect them to form the basis of what they see from Hollywood.

Most teams spend a weekend in a haunted home or location with planted cameras to capture evidence, and then go home and create a YouTube show, while nothing else is mentioned about the family who may live in the home, or the workers that occupy that haunted space daily. When it comes to some of these locations and cases, maybe people just aren't looking at these cases thoroughly, and maybe they are too quick to base everything on capturing an epic piece of evidence to show instead of working with those claiming to be affected by these hauntings, on a spiritual, emotional, and physical level.

Demonologist Carl L. Johnson, famous for his

investigative work on the Perron Family estate from the Ed and Lorraine Warren Case Files that inspired the movie *The Conjuring*, wrote a book called *Shadow Realms Demonology Handbook*. In his work, he encourages his readers to look at the idea of negative spirits differently. It's a collection of firsthand accounts in different cases in which he endeavors to branch out beyond the set standards of what is traditionally known as "demonology;" to "think outside the box" and ponder new theories on negative spirits, demons, and the shadow realms for which they dwell. He writes a quote from a spirit that he received firsthand that alludes to how a negative entity can attach itself to a person.

"I will drive you mad … I will drive you mad with death and gloom; I will drive you out, but it will be too late because you will be dead," he writes in his work.

This idea of negative entity attachments is nothing new. But to acknowledge the existence of demons is to acknowledge a host of other things as well, such as elementals, land spirits, fae, and a host of other spiritual phenomena, such as angels, spirit guides, etc. When looking at the unknown, it is important to remember that there are no experts in the field. The unknown will always be unknown, and only for those who are in spirit to know.

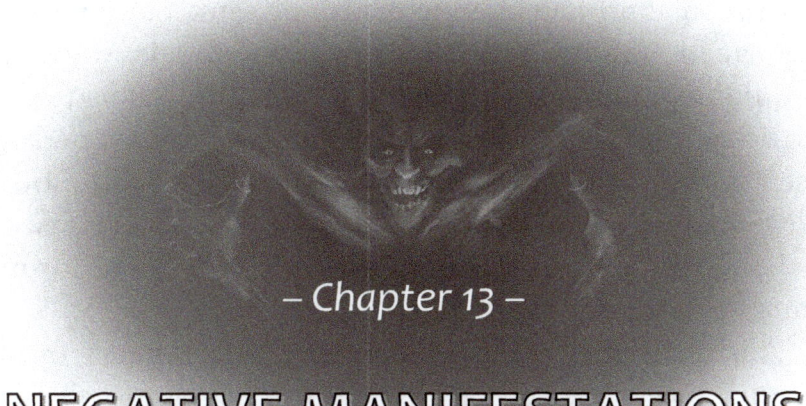

– Chapter 13 –

NEGATIVE MANIFESTATIONS

"And can you teach your body emotionally what it would feel like to believe in this way . . . to be empowered . . . to be moved by your own greatness . . . to be invincible . . . to have courage . . . to be in love with life . . . to feel unlimited . . . to live as if your prayers are already answered?"
— Joe Dispenza

Beliefs about demons and their behavior vary widely across cultures, religions, and belief systems. In many cases, the idea that demons target people who are vulnerable, suffering, or facing difficulties might be rooted in the concept of evil entities exploiting moments of weakness, such as vices. Because of this, oppression, possession, and the capacity for negative entity attachments are most often associated with people who are living in poverty, come from broken homes, or face other socio-economic challenges.

In the documentary *Demon House*, for instance, the negative attachment was associated with a single-parent family living in the economically depressed town of Gary,

Indiana. In almost all cases like this, the same pattern can be ascertained. The famous Italian exorcist Gabriele Amorth, in his autobiography *An Exorcist Tells His Story*, claims to have performed thousands of exorcisms and conducted personal case studies on hundreds of individuals who sought deliverance from "evil influence." In each of these cases in his book, the person was always a victim of some form of trauma, abuse, or poverty.

This leads me to discuss negative attachments from a personal level. The call of the void reaches out to all of us, through some sort of vice, or life challenge that must be overcome in life. Though it's not easy, the most successful way of overcoming any oppression is when a person decides to take back their life and to move forward in light. But this comes down to the person themselves. They must decide to make certain changes.

In the last chapter, I quoted the words of a priest and theologian from his work, *The Great Exorcism*, originally released in 1915.

"An insidious, sneaking enemy, who enters the very heart of you, and pretends to be you, with the lie that it is you, – you are accusing yourself – this influence cannot be thrown out or cast down by your own strength," he states, suggesting that, without the help of others, one cannot overcome such negative entities. I have experienced the exact opposite of this and believe that a person must decide to overcome it.

Similarly, this theme is also played out in many different cultures. For instance, in the Navajo Nation, the traditions used to cure someone of "ghost illness" involve counseling from the shaman or healer of the community. These shamans are trained from a young age to work with both the spirit of the afflicted and the spirits causing the affliction.

Most often, ghost illness is believed to be caused by the afflicted individual who inadvertently invites the spirit of the deceased or negative energy into their own lives through various methods. The most common cause is the failure of a person to let go of a deceased loved one. They hold on to the spirit of the deceased. To relieve the person of this illness, ceremonies are performed to help them let go of their loved one. However, in the end, the person being afflicted must make the decision to let go–to heal themselves from their loss.

To reference the episode from *The Holzer Files* again, "The Devil in Texas", the reason the case by Hans Holzer in Tyler Texas is reopened was because a woman named Lydia in Missouri reaches out to Dave Schrader with similar paranormal phenomena going on in her life, and who believed she was being physically attacked, as well as her kids. The investigators, Dave Schrader, Cindy Kaza and Shane Pittman return to Texas to gauge what they were up against with the new case in Missouri first. When they finally show up at the location of the new case, they find that the entity was attached to Lydia and would not manifest itself until she was part of the investigation.

Given the nature of this case, I'm almost certain that much was left unsaid. Again, this case bore so many similarities to my own. Once the team concluded that she was indeed afflicted and affected by a negative entity with a strong hold on her, questions arose. Learning about her abusive past and current life stressors, we must consider whether Lydia was drawing this energy to herself through negative thought manifestation. Are we dealing with dark forces, an external force, or something within us that possesses such powers?

In a later interview with Dave Schrader about this case,

he said, "I think this case was an interesting marriage of self and supernatural. Sometimes the demons in our head are just as real as the supernatural kind, and we become our own worst enemy."

This case is one of my favorite paranormal television shows because it was about the client and the personal healing this individual had to undergo to overcome the haunting she was experiencing. Referred to as psychological projection, Lydia had a defense mechanism of "alterity," in which "inside" content was mistakenly perceived as coming from the "outside."

This projection originated from a background of childhood abuse. This is not to say that spiritual oppression from a negative entity was taking place in this case, because Lydia did have an attachment. Individuals with abusive backgrounds can become a feeding ground for negative entities, especially if someone like Lydia, who had psychic abilities, is involved.

It was discovered that Lydia had psychic abilities, which attracted these energies to her in the first place. The turning point came when Dave Schrader advised Lydia to stand her ground and reclaim her life.

My belief system differs from that of the Christian concepts of demonic and negative attachments in that I believe that all humanity has free will. The quote, "The soul becomes dyed with the color of its thoughts," by Roman emperor Marcus Aurelius in his *Meditations on Stoic Philosophy*, is a powerful reminder that our thoughts greatly influence who we are. It suggests that our inner world—our thoughts, beliefs, and attitudes—shapes our outer reality, including our actions, reactions, and overall demeanor. If we are living in victim based, fear-based ways of life, we become prone to negative outcomes.

In the almond orchard case in California, I followed up with the client several times after initially clearing the inside of her house with advice on taking back her space. She was still having problems in the home and continued to believe that her life was being oppressed, and she was experiencing deep depression from her circumstances. Sadly, she is still not able to overcome it. But it leaves me with the belief about such cases, that there is only so much anyone can do to help someone overcome oppression.

Like addictions, abusive relationships, and other such life obstacles, there comes a point when the person must decide to heal themselves and to move forward. This comes in the form of meditation, sometimes counseling, sometimes cutting out of our lives what no longer serves us, changing mindsets and thought processes, healing from abuses, and letting go of the past. Some deep amends must be made to move forward in light, but it's a process worth taking to heal the self.

In my own life, the oppression stopped for a while when I moved out of the house. However, they would continue to manifest again in different times of my life, most often when I let my guard down, become distracted with life's problems, or succumb to my own vices, such as depression. It's one of those things that can't be completely kicked, but controlling emotions and thoughts, particularly as someone with psychic abilities, and to allow myself healing goes a long way.

The intricate interplay between our thoughts and our lives is a profound testament to the power of the mind. Thoughts serve as the seeds from which our actions, emotions, and decisions bloom. They shape our perceptions, influencing how we interpret the world around us and guiding our responses to various situations. Positive thoughts often cultivate confidence, resilience, and optimism, propelling us toward achievement and growth. Conversely, negative thoughts can constrict our potential, fostering self-doubt, anxiety, and limitations. The mind's ability to direct our focus and attitude is pivotal; it can determine whether we embrace opportunities or shy away from challenges.

Another aspect of this is discerning other energy from your own. Those with psychic abilities often draw energy to themselves and can take on emotion and energies that are outside of themselves. How often do you meet other psychics who are often surrounded by constant drama? I truly believe they manifest this energy by picking up everything else around them. But this doesn't have to be the case. We choose what energy we are going to react to, to manifest and to be affected by, either consciously or subconsciously. Through self-reflection and meditation, we can learn to discern and let go of what isn't our own energy.

ABOUT THE AUTHOR

 C.L. Thomas was born in Pittsburgh, Pennsylvania. After graduating from Belmont University, she moved to Nashville to pursue a career in communications and photojournalism, where she lived for over ten years. As a fine arts photographer and writer, C.L. travels widely every year exploring various afterlife research, OBEs, metaphysics, folklore, and paranormal events and groups. She has written many articles and maintains a blog on legends, folklore, magic, and supernatural stories. C.L. is also the host for the Small Town Tales Podcast. Currently, she resides in Las Vegas, Nevada, with her beloved golden retriever and Maine Coon cat.
.

Other titles from Haunted Road Media:

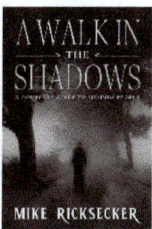

A WALK IN THE SHADOWS

Shadow people are some of the most mysterious entities in the known universe, and Mike Ricksecker has experienced many, starting with a tall, dark humanoid figure that appeared in his room as a child. *A Walk In The Shadows* explores the secrets of the dark while unveiling an enigmatic world feared by many and misunderstood by most.

DAYS OF THE DEAD

Are you brave enough to spend every day of the year with ghosts? Paranormal reporter Sylvia Shults has collected 366 ghost stories, one for every single day of the year, and has detailed them in this ambitious work. There's a story for your birthday. There's a story for your pet's birthday. There's a story to make every day spooky. Open the cover and peek inside - if you dare.

WHERE THE PARTY NEVER ENDED

The Old Baraboo Inn in Baraboo, Wisconsin, is one of the Midwest's most haunted places. Home to a lively cast of ghostly characters, as many as 30 spirits may haunt the Inn. In the last 150 years, the Inn has also been home to more than one saloon, restaurant, hotel, brewery, boarding house, billiard hall, and bar, and has long been speculated to have once been a brothel, gambling house, and Prohibition-era speakeasy as well.

ENCOUNTERS WITH THE PARANORMAL

Almost everyone has a ghost story. Real people. Real stories. Read about haunted houses and vehicles, experiences during paranormal investigations, visits from relatives that have passed on, pets reacting to the paranormal, psychic experiences, and conversations with full-bodied apparitions. *Encounters with the Paranormal* reveals personal stories of the supernatural, exploring the realm beyond the veil.

www.ingramcontent.com/pod-product-compliance
Lightning Source LLC
Chambersburg PA
CBHW071512120626
46550CB00006B/2203